ESSENTIAL RESEARCH SKILLS

Also in the HarperCollins Essential Series

Essential Accountancy and Finance
Bijon Kar

Essential Business Studies
Stephen Barnes

Essential Government and Politics
Jim Cordell

Essential Marketing
Tony Proctor

Essential Mechanics
Owen Elbourn

Essential Practical Psychology
Keith Maglennon

Essential Psychology
G.C. Davenport

Essential Information Technology
Tony Berk

Essential GCSE Business Studies
Renée Huggett

ESSENTIAL RESEARCH SKILLS

Val Bailey, Geoff Bemrose, Sharon Goddard, Ron Impey, Erica Joslyn and Jen Mackness

Collins Educational

An Imprint of HarperCollins*Publishers*

Published in 1995 by Collins Educational
An imprint of HarperCollins *Publishers*
77–85 Fulham Palace Road
Hammersmith
London W6 8JB

Reprinted 1996

ISBN 0–00–322356–6

British Library Cataloguing-in-publication data
A catalogue record for this book is available from the British Library

Cover design by Ridgeway Associates
Typeset by Harper Phototypesetters Limited
Northampton, England
Printed in Great Britain by Scotprint, Musselburgh.

Contents

Foreword

Every book in the Essential Series is designed carefully to put you in control of your own learning.

When using this book, you will not only cover the key elements of your course but you will also benefit from the author's use of modern learning techniques, with the result that you will make the best possible use of your time.

This book includes the following features.

- An introductory section at the beginning of each chapter, focusing your attention on its contents and telling you exactly what you should have learned by the end of the chapter. These are your 'learning objectives'.

- End of chapter reviews, giving you a synopsis of the most important points you should have learned.

- Notes in the margin of the text, where the author takes the role of a tutor: picking out key ideas and highlighting important concepts.

- A wide variety of activities that allow you to learn by applying the ideas in the text.

Learning is not easy; nobody learns without effort. However, if you use this book effectively, you will not only succeed in your course and assessment, but you will also enjoy the experience of learning.

Acknowledgements

The author and publishers would like to thank the following:

Her Majesty's Stationary Office (HMSO) for information about households with regular use of a car and car ownership from the *General Household Survey and Social Trends 1993* (Chapter 8, p. 106).

Routledge for permission to reproduce the back cover of and pages from *Come on Down: Popular Media Culture in Post-War Britain*, edited by Dominic Strinati and Stephen Wagg (1992) (Chapter 9, pp. 121–6).

Suffolk College Library for permission to reproduce the front cover of their Library Guide, and their Book Request/Reservation and Journal Request cards (Chapter 8, pp. 104, 112 and 113).

How to use this book

Who is this book for?
- It is designed for all students who have to carry out research or an enquiry as part of their course, whether the research is into human behaviour, animals, businesses or the environment. Such research is becoming more and more common, especially in courses such as GNVQ, where assignments are a central feature of the course.

What will this book do?
- It will take you step by step through the stages of designing and carrying out a research project or assignment.
- It will give you advice and examples on many different kinds of projects covering a range of research areas.
- It will enable you to build up confidence and develop the skills necessary to complete a successful research project.

How will it do this?
- It is a work book. That means it offers you activities to do that will help you understand the research process.
- You can either work through the book completely on your own or you can use it as a text book within your course of study.

AN INTRODUCTION TO THE BOOK

The book is designed to follow the normal stages of a project, from start to finish. But you will also find that individual chapters can be studied on their own.

Instructions are clearly given to take you from one stage of the research process to the next. These stages range from defining a suitable area for research to the final completion of the project.

Problems and pitfalls are identified together with suggestions for overcoming them.

WHAT WILL I GET OUT OF THIS BOOK?

This book will give you:

- the chance to get an excellent grade for your research project;
- the confidence to do your own project, which will increase as you use the book and complete the activities;

- the skills to plan, develop and successfully carry out a project;
- personal transferable skills, such as time management, which can be included in your personal profile or record of achievement;
- if you are following a GNVQ course, evidence for the GNVQ core skills of Communication, Information Technology and Application of Number;
- opportunities to organize your study time and to follow through an enquiry or assignment with relatively little help from your tutor – these are important criteria for achieving a Merit or Distinction in GNVQ;
- knowledge of the research process which will help you in your current project, in other projects in the future, and in understanding the results of other people's research.

HOW DO I USE THIS BOOK?

As a workbook

Using the book as a workbook means organizing your reading of the book to coincide with the stages of your own research. The logical sequence of the book will help to guide you through the stages, and the activities will help you develop the project. You should keep and use your responses to the planning activities since these will help you plan your way through your project.

As a text book

Using the book as a text books means selecting appropriate areas or chapters to increase your understanding of a particular issue or aspect of the research. You should use the contents page, the index and the margin notes to guide you.

Where are you now?

 Locate yourself on the algorithm on the opposite page.

Now that you have located yourself in relation to your project, you should know which chapter you need to refer to in the book.

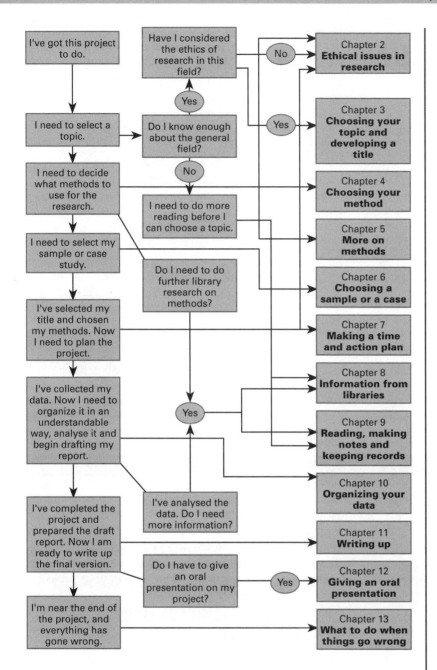

Figure 1.1 Algorithm showing which chapter to refer to for each stage of your project

2 *Ethical issues in research*

► In this book, we usually use the term 'participant in' rather than 'subject' or 'object of' research.

► **Research ethics** refer to the responsibility of the researcher to make sure that the participants are not harmed by the research.

► **Ethics** are principles or values pertaining to rules of good and bad conduct. Ethical behaviour is good or right behaviour. Unethical behaviour is bad or wrong behaviour.

WHAT ARE RESEARCH ETHICS?

If your project involves investigation into the lives of people or animals you must protect them, as far as possible, from any harm that may result from your research. The purpose of this chapter is to help you to understand and recognize the possible harmful effects of research. It will also enable you to use a variety of means to ensure that your participants will have confidence in your project.

To cause harm or distress to the participants is unacceptable and is considered **unethical**. Ethical judgements can be applied to anyone and everyone. One of the main purposes of ethics is to urge everyone to do good and right by others.

Ethics is used in research to judge the behaviour of the researcher and the consequences of the research. Ethical judgements can be made about past or present behaviour as well as about actions and activities planned for the future.

> The conduct of researchers lies on a continuum ranging from the clearly unethical to the clearly ethical.

The first part of this chapter explores some common ethical concerns in research and will help you to use established methods to avoid ethical problems. In planning your project you may wish to develop your own code of ethics. The second part of this chapter will help you to design a code that is appropriate to your project.

Ethics and morals

The purpose of ethics is to guide individuals to make decisions when there is a moral question of whether an action is right or wrong. Ethics provides a set of rules by which to judge the consequences of actions. Whether consequences are judged to be moral or immoral depends upon the values held by the researcher. There are many views about what values must be reflected in research but they all involve creating a balance between, on the one hand, giving the highest moral priority to the welfare and benefit of the participants and, on the other, giving the highest moral priority to the benefits of increasing knowledge through research.

Prioritizing the rights of participants

Some researchers place the highest value on the rights of the individuals or animals being researched. According to this view, if the effects of research are potentially harmful the question must be asked: 'Should this research be done?' It is argued that individuals should not be used as a means of obtaining information without any regard for their welfare. Those who are researched are believed to have certain rights that must not be ignored, even if the research is considered extremely important. According to this view, researchers should never treat those they research simply as a means to gain knowledge but always as individuals with rights. In this view there can be no ethical justification for research where there is a risk of harming or upsetting the participants. Even if no harm actually came to the participants, taking the risk would be considered unethical.

Prioritizing the results of the research

By contrast, some researchers place the highest value on the results of research. This view can sometimes be used to justify the methods used even where they involve deception or harm to some individuals. The benefits of research can therefore be considered more important than individuals' rights, especially when the research promises to benefit a larger number of people than those actually studied. The researcher may feel that conducting a particular project is more important than protecting the rights of individual participants. Similarly, researchers may consider it important to publish certain information even if it means publishing without the permission of participants.

(ACT) *A moral dilemma*

We would like you to think about the previous two paragraphs by looking at the following moral dilemma.

A drug company has developed a new drug that its

▶ A **code of ethics** is a set of regulations guiding the behaviour of researchers. Codes also let participants know how they will be protected if they agree to take part in the project.

▶ Ethical problems are moral problems. The terms 'ethical' and 'moral' may be used interchangeably.

▶ Some researchers place the overriding value on the rights of the participants; others on the importance of research findings.

▶ Researchers who take this view may choose only to do research that benefits those who are being researched.

researchers believe will cure a particularly serious disease. To test the drug properly it is thought necessary to have two groups of patients with the disease, some of whom (the experimental group) will receive the new drug and some of whom (the control group) will receive a widely used drug that is known to be of limited effectiveness. The patients, their doctors and their nurses will not know which drug has been administered. Only the researchers will know this.

► The procedure described in this activity is in standard use in drug research. It is called a 'double-blind' research procedure.

To use this method of finding out whether the new drug is effective and safe the researchers will have to:

- withhold information from the patients – overriding their right to know what drugs they are taking;
- deprive some patients of treatment with a drug that is thought to be effective, while giving it to others;
- put some patients at risk from taking a new and untested drug while not subjecting others to the same risk.

First think about this situation as if only the rights and welfare of the patients were to be considered. Would this be an ethical piece of research? Give reasons for your answer.

Now, think of the situation as if the main concern were the benefits of introducing an effective new drug to hundreds of thousands of patients in the future and/or preventing a dangerous drug from being launched. Would this be an ethical piece of research? Give reasons for your answer.

All research is full of difficult moral, or ethical, dilemmas. The dilemmas are made particularly complex because it is often difficult to predict what benefits the research might have or what harm it might do. Researchers try to reach an ethical compromise between avoiding harm to some people and doing good to others.

► The kind of research you will be doing as a student will rarely be of benefit to anyone except yourself. Therefore you will need to concentrate most on avoiding harm to those who are involved in your research.

WHY ETHICS IN RESEARCH?

Since the 1940s, concern for the welfare of participants has become an important feature of research. Over the last fifty years, mechanisms and guidelines have been developed to protect participants from loss of individual rights.

For researchers, one of the most important tasks is to maintain respect for participants, to be sensitive to what could go wrong and to safeguard the rights of participants. The ways in which participants may be harmed by research may vary according to the kind of research. For example, there is a greater risk of inflicting physical harm through medical research than through social research. On the other hand, medical and social research are equally capable of causing social and psychological distress.

Benefits to researchers and benefits to participants

Consider the following case study and make two lists. One list should show how the researchers were affected by the research; the other should show the effects on participants.

CASE STUDY

In 1958, Vidich and Bensman carried out a field study of a small town in upstate New York. This study was intended to explore the foundations of social life in a community. Before the project began, the town's residents were assured by the researchers that no individual would be identified in published reports. To reassure the residents, the researchers developed a code of ethics specially for the project. However, when Vidich and Bensman's work was published, although individuals were given fictitious names, some were identifiable and described in ways that were damaging to them, causing embarrassment and distress.

Following the publication of this study, other social scientists felt that the authors had gone too far and had damaged the town's image of itself. Moreover, the authors were judged to have broken the research bargain they had made with the town's residents.

Potential dangers for participants

It is impossible to list all the possible negative or undesirable effects of research. However some of the most common ones are that participants may:

- lose privacy because of the collection of certain types of information about them or their circumstances;
- become embarrassed or legally liable if private information is made public;
- suffer anxiety because of what they may be asked to do;
- suffer actual changes in their characteristics: for example, deterioration of their physical health;
- be put under pressure to participate in activities when they would rather not.

For these reasons the protection of the rights of participants is an essential feature of any research project, no matter how small.

Protecting the rights of participants

The protection of participants' rights begins with their individual human right to privacy, to confidentiality and to consent or refuse to participate in any research project.

Privacy

Participants have a **right to privacy**. To uphold this right, researchers are required to seek the permission of participants before they collect information from or about them.

▶ **The research bargain** is the agreement that researchers make with the people they study. Promising confidentiality or anonymity is a common part of the research bargain in social-scientific and psychological research.

▶ The **right to privacy** is the freedom of each individual to decide the type and amount of information about themselves that can be shared with or withheld from others.

▶ An ethical problem is created when a researcher publishes information about a participant that the participant would not want published. When this happens the participant will experience a loss of his or her right to privacy.

This need to seek permission to collect information can pose practical problems for researchers. On the one hand the researcher cannot use personal information about participants without their permission. On the other hand researchers are sometimes unlikely to get this permission, especially if they seek sensitive information. To overcome this problem, most researchers promise anonymity and confidentiality to participants.

Anonymity

You can safeguard the privacy of your participants by allowing them to contribute to your project **anonymously.** This means that participants will not be required to give a name. If the information is given anonymously then the privacy of participants is assured because their identity is unknown. In order for participants to be anonymous, neither you nor any other person should be able to identify the source of any data. Data that cannot be traced back to a person has very little chance of causing harm to that person. Data collected in this way can be used free from the threat of harm or embarrassment to anyone.

▶ You may have noticed that in television documentaries the faces of participants are sometimes obscured, and sometimes their voices are disguised using an electronic device.

Being anonymous offers the participant the opportunity to speak and to act free from the threat of being identified. If participants know they cannot be identified, they often feel more positive about taking part in the project. In addition, if they are not personally identified, participants can be reassured that any further contact with the researcher is unlikely. If your data is collected by means of a postal questionnaire, it is easy to ensure anonymity. If, on the other hand, you use face-to-face interviews, anonymity is much more difficult. If you use this method of gathering information, you will need to provide more reassurance to your participants. They are more likely to feel threatened or exposed to harmful effects, especially when the topic is of a sensitive nature.

 Protecting anonymity

Anonymity is maintained in a postal survey provided that no identifying names or numbers are used in questionnaires. In this case the researcher has no personal contact with the participant and cannot easily identify the participant. On the other hand a participant taking part in a personal face-to-face interview cannot be anonymous to the researcher. How would you protect the anonymity of your participant, using the interview method of data collection?

Confidentiality

While anonymity refers to the identity of individuals, **confidentiality** refers to the information and data they provide. In social and medical research, anonymity is closely linked to confidentiality. If the name of the participant were made public then the information would no longer be confidential. A breach of privacy about identity increases the possibility of a breach of confidentiality.

▶ Every researcher has an obligation to keep information confidential.

Participants in research are commonly reassured that the information they provide will be treated as confidential. In projects where participants are known to the researcher they may be reassured that the researcher will not publicly reveal either their identity or their information. Every researcher has a strict moral and professional obligation to keep information confidential.

Confidentiality applies to all types of data and includes photographs and information obtained through casual conversations. Sometimes it may not be possible to keep information completely confidential but it is necessary to use as many safeguards as possible. Permission must always be obtained before you release this kind of confidential data.

When permission is being requested for the use of materials such as photographs, participants must be given information about how far these will be made public. Participants have a right to know how far confidentiality can be guaranteed. In the case of photographs it is difficult to offer complete guarantees of confidentiality but efforts can be made to reduce identifying features. In addition, participants have a right to know your plans for publishing the results of the project.

The question of confidentiality will also influence how much information an informant is prepared to give you. For example, no business manager should give you details of company budgets, financial forecasts or marketing plans. It is unlikely that a business would answer questions about whether it is observing all the rules about health and safety. An officer in charge of a residential home should not be asked for information about individual residents.

The Data Protection Act

The Data Protection Act covers the storage of data about individuals by means of computers (databases, disks, tapes, etc.). It does not cover data stored in manual systems, such as card indexes or files of paper.

It is designed to protect confidential information falling into the wrong hands or being disclosed by accident. Therefore in principle it only applies to records containing information that is not already public and that can be identified with specific individuals. Thus if you stored information about people but each person was only identified by a code number in the computer files, or if you stored information about people identified by name but only recorded their addresses, then it is probable that these files would not fall under the Act.

The key question for you to ask is this:

If the computer system were broken into, could someone extract information on identifiable individuals and, if so, would this information be confidential information?

▶ The Data Protection Act will affect you if you plan to use a computer to store information about identifiable individuals.

▶ Take care in deciding whether the information you are saving to disk is public or confidential. If you were known to be researching users of illegal drugs, then just saving their names and addresses on your computer could incriminate them.

If the answer is 'yes' to both questions, you will be committing an offence by storing the data without registering your system under the Data Protection Act. At the time of writing it costs £56 to register, plus the possible cost of buying and fitting security devices to your system.

You will probably find it more convenient to avoid the need to register by not filing anything on the computer that can be attributed to identifiable individuals.

You can find out more about the Data Protection Act by writing to:

> The Data Protection Registrar
> Springfield House, Water Lane
> Wilmslow, Cheshire, SK9 5AX
> telephone: 0625–535777

Consent

There is now wide acceptance of the view that research involving human subjects should normally be performed only with their **consent.** Consent is especially important when participants are exposed to substantial risks, such as risks of injury in sports research.

▶ **Informed consent** means that the research participant has enough information to be able to make a sensible decision about whether to be involved in the research. It is the researcher's obligation to supply this information.

The principle of informed consent should not be an absolute requirement of all research. Although desirable, it is not necessary in studies where no danger or risk is involved. The more serious the risk to research participants, the greater becomes the obligation to obtain informed consent.

Each participant has a right to decide whether to participate in a research project, and he or she should always be given the opportunity to choose. When participants have voluntarily agreed to take part in a project, the legal liability of the researcher is reduced. However, consent can only be given if participants are sure about what they are agreeing to. This raises many questions such as: 'How do we know that a person understands the information that is given?' and 'How much information should be given?'

▶ 'Informed consent' has been formally defined in the **Nuremberg Code**.

The Nuremberg Code

The Nuremberg Code, developed after the Second World War, provides a definition of informed consent that now acts as a guideline for many researchers. The code states that:

> the person involved should have the legal capacity to give consent; should be so situated as to be able to exercise free power of choice, without the intervention of any element of force, fraud, deceit, over-reaching, or other ulterior form of constraint or coercion.

Although there is no clear method of obtaining informed consent, the Nuremberg Code identifies four important conditions. If followed closely, these conditions will help you to ensure that you will not mislead your participants.

Condition 1

The participants must be competent to make decisions for themselves. Those considered incompetent include young children and people suffering from mental disorders. When such participants may receive benefit from their involvement in a research project it may be appropriate for guardians and parents to make a decision for them.

Condition 2

The individuals must freely volunteer to participate. This may be a particular issue in institutional settings such as schools and hospitals since participants may be influenced by the involvement of persons in positions of authority. For example, a student who has been asked by the head teacher to participate may feel obliged to do so.

Condition 3

The individual must be given full information. Consent is only adequate when it is given voluntarily and after the participant has been fully informed. Consent that is given voluntarily but on the basis of wrong or inadequate information does not fulfil the conditions of informed consent. Neither does consent that is fully informed but given involuntarily.

▶ In practice, it is very difficult to get voluntary and fully informed consent.

Condition 4

The individual must fully understand what is being requested. An elaborate description of a project, even if it is provided in non-technical language, may be difficult to understand. Keep explanations simple, as brief as possible, but still truthful.

 Applying the Nuremberg code

Try applying the conditions of the Nuremberg Code to the following three research proposals:

(a) research into the movements of rail passengers from the platform entrance to the train, where the main kind of data to be used is video recording;

(b) research into the experience of young job-seekers, where the main kind of data will come from tape-recorded interviews;

(c) the medical research example given in the first activity in this chapter (p. 5–6).

The practice of obtaining informed consent is the most commonly used solution to the problem of how to promote research without encroaching upon individual rights. In principle, if all four conditions associated with informed consent are satisfied, you can be reasonably confident that you have given appropriate attention to the basic rights of your participants. In practice, as you saw in the activity above, the importance of applying the code and the ease of applying it vary for different kinds of research.

Research with few ethical implications

Some kinds of research project present almost no ethical dilemmas. Most of these are where the data for research is already 'public' in some way. Examples might include:

- research on the content of popular newspapers or television programmes;
- research based on data published in company reports;
- research based on data provided by a business in response to your letter asking for information and explaining how you will use it;
- a study of decision-making from observing council meetings that are open to the public;
- research on ancient field patterns from old maps, contemporary maps or site visits;
- research on the kinds of shops to be found in different kinds of shopping centres.

Some kinds of research may present ethical problems that are both minor and virtually impossible to deal with. For example, there is some invasion of privacy involved in making a video tape of pedestrians in a town centre – security cameras do this all the time. But the task of analysing such a tape would be impossible if it depended on first tracking down and obtaining the permission of everyone who appears on it. Of course, the ethical problems would be greater if you wanted to publish clips from the tape.

▶ Sometimes, obtaining consent is impracticable and unnecessary.

Advantages of ethics in your research

Trust and cooperation

The success or failure of your research depends very much on help and cooperation from other people, as participants are sources of information. The more they trust you, the more helpful they will be. Participants need to know that your project poses no threat to them and that their participation is valued. One of the best ways to demonstrate this is to show participants that your research design takes account of their rights and safety.

If you seek and obtain consent from your participants, they will be more likely to develop an interest in assisting you with your project. If you explain to them the purpose of the project and the methods you will use to maintain confidentiality, they will be reassured of your commitment to their needs and rights. If you ask permission from participants before using and publishing data, they will feel that they have some control over the information. By seeking their permission you will also demonstrate that you are committed to protecting their privacy.

Participants should feel valued by the researcher. If you are able to tell participants how their contribution will add to your study, they may feel more comfortable about taking part.

In addition, of course, by paying attention to ethics you will reduce the risk of harming others, avoid criticism for your actions, and keep a clear conscience.

Remember:

> The greater the sensitivity of the information you are asking for, the more you will need to protect and reassure your participants.

► If you ignore ethics you risk causing harm and inviting criticism.

RESEARCHING ANIMALS AND THE ENVIRONMENT

Animal rights

So far we have discussed research as if the subjects were always people. But many student research projects involve animals, plants or the environment in a more general way. Many of the same ethical principles apply. First there is the question of balancing the harm that may be caused to the research subjects with the good that may be done by the results of the research. With animals there is an important ethical issue: the question of what rights animals have and whether benefit to humans always outweighs harm to animals. In the past many researchers behaved as if it were always justifiable to sacrifice the welfare of animals when doing so gave some benefit to human beings, however small. It is still the case that tens of thousands of animals a year are experimented on and killed in order to test drugs, cosmetics, weapons, new surgical techniques and so on. With the development of the animal rights movement this has become an important political issue.

► Since student research rarely results in great benefit to humans (apart from the researcher), harming animals in student research can almost never be justified.

Animals, of course, cannot give informed consent to being involved in research. The researcher has therefore to take more – not less – responsibility for their welfare. Issues similar to those of privacy, anonymity and confidentiality may sometimes arise where animals are being studied in their natural habitat. For example, someone studying badger behaviour would need to be careful about disclosing the site of a badger sett, and anyone studying animal behaviour in the wild would need to be careful not to disturb the natural behaviour of the animals.

► Examination boards usually supply codes of practice for student research with animals. If your research is going to involve animals you should check to see whether the examination board provides such a code of practice.

The Countryside Code
The Countryside Code is a simple and sensible code of practice you might use if your research involves field studies in the countryside. It includes references to the law covering protected species of plants and animals. You can obtain a copy from your local Wildlife Trust.

► When considering the problem of gaining access, you must also consider the issues of confidentiality and privacy.

► On participant observation see Chapter 5.

GAINING ACCESS TO INFORMATION

In order to research and collect data it is first necessary to gain access to sources of information. Your project may involve respondents, participants or literature such as historical documents. These sources are not always easily available to researchers and access may have to be carefully negotiated.

Access to research information may be refused: for example, information about some organizations and professional groups. The more powerful the group or organization, the more difficult it is to gain access for research. A method sometimes used to negotiate access to this kind of confidential information is to offer the 'top management' of the organization the right to review the project manuscript before it is published.

There are also non-powerful groups that researchers may find hard to gain access to. For example, access to black communities may be relatively closed to white researchers. Similarly, access to homeless or unemployed people may be relatively closed to those who do not belong to these groups. The most common method of research for this area is the use of participant observation.

Covert research

Care must be taken when using participant observation, especially when researchers in the field pretend to be something that they are not, such as homeless or drug-dependent. Many ethical issues are raised by the use of this kind of deception where participants are secretly observed or asked disguised questions. The most serious consideration is that certain forms of deception may invade the privacy of the participant. Deception by the researcher violates the right of participants to make an informed choice – or in the case of secret observation to make any sort of choice – about whether their opinions and beliefs are communicated to others.

 An ethical dilemma in participant observation research

A student has decided to study the behaviour of people at rave parties. She is certain that if she asks the organizer's permission to do this, she will be refused. Yet if she buys a ticket, she has every right to attend the party. Her research technique is observing and chatting. These are things she would do, though for different purposes, if she merely attended as a partygoer. She is worried about the ethics of doing this without telling those she observes and chats to, but feels that if she does tell them they may not respond to her naturally, and that the bouncers might throw her out. How would you advise her to proceed?

Other research information may be more open and available to researchers; for example from friends, neighbours or family. In these circumstances it may become even more important to ensure confidentiality, privacy and trust.

GAINING ACCESS TO RESEARCH SETTINGS

The setting of a research project may vary from being totally private to entirely public. Whatever the setting, you are likely to need someone's permission to use the location you have chosen.

A home is one of the most private settings, and entering the home of others without their consent is forbidden by law. Door-to-door research should not be done by students as this may cause distress to residents and requires complex notifications to the police and the local authority.

It is always possible to seek information by conducting a street survey. It is not usually necessary to obtain anyone's permission for this but it is sensible to inform the local police in advance, if only to check that you will not be standing on private property, which can include some shopping centres. The police may ask for details of your survey. You do not have to supply these, but it is sensible to inform them of the purpose of the study, the expected location, the time and date of the survey and the identities of those involved. When conducting a street survey it is essential to carry proper identification, and you should take care to behave in a non-threatening, polite and friendly manner.

 Confidentiality, privacy and consent in a street survey

> How should confidentiality, privacy and consent be ensured in a street survey? Write down precisely what you would say to someone whom you approach for information.

Some research will be conducted on premises that are privately owned or open only to certain people: for example, a workplace, day-centre, sports centre or school. In these cases it will nearly always be necessary to secure permission from the owner to conduct the research.

WORKING WITH CHILDREN

Projects involving children require special attention since there are both legal and ethical considerations. Children are particularly vulnerable to exploitation and the most important ethical consideration is that of consent. If you wish to work with children you *must* first obtain the permission of the parent or guardian of each child included in your research. It is sensible to obtain written consent in order to prevent misunderstandings or any breach of the rights of the child. However, verbal consent may sometimes be enough. Whether you obtain written or verbal consent will depend

▶ The Criminal Justice Act, which came into force in November 1994, changed the law of trespass. Trespass, which necessarily involved damage to property, was previously a civil matter between the landowner and the trespasser. Many kinds of trespass are now a criminal offence and it is no longer necessary to cause damage to commit the offence of trespass.

▶ Parental permission is legally required for research involving children under the age of 17.

upon the type of project and the kind of observations you wish to make. You will need to take advice from your supervisor.

Parents and guardians must give consent for the research, whatever the setting. Therefore, even if your project setting is in a nursery or school you will still need to obtain parental permission for your project.

You must also get permission if you wish to use photographs or any other information that may identify the child. All data relating to the child and family must be kept confidential at all times and may only be made public with the permission of the parent or guardian.

In order to be granted permission to include children in your project you will need to reassure the parent or guardian of the safety and confidentiality of your project. If you have designed an ethical code of conduct for your project, this can be shared with parents, guardians, supervisors and others, and will demonstrate your commitment to safety, confidentiality and consent.

▶ In schools or nurseries you will need to seek permission from the head of the school or nursery (and perhaps from the local education authority) as well as from the parents.

WORKING WITH VOLUNTEER PARTICIPANTS

Using volunteers carries specific problems.

▶ The use of volunteers raises issues not only of ethics but also of representativeness – see also Chapter 6.

- When recruiting volunteers you must avoid making promises that cannot be carried out. It is unethical to raise false hopes.
- Full information should include potential benefits as well as possible damaging effects. If there is a possibility of damage or injury, it can be argued that the research should not be done at all.
- Projects that rely solely on volunteers may inadvertently exclude certain individuals from participating. In practice, volunteers tend to be white, better educated, middle class, and more sociable than non-volunteers. The use of volunteers can create a situation where some groups are being discriminated against, such as people from working-class and ethnic minority backgrounds and less sociable people.

APPROACHING COMMERCIAL ORGANIZATIONS

Writing a request for information

Many student researchers, especially those taking vocational courses such as GNVQ, will find themselves writing to business people and commercial organizations to ask for information. All such organizations are finding that they are receiving more and more enquiries of this kind. From their point of view, every such letter means time spent preparing an answer, and perhaps money spent on materials such as leaflets and information packs. When writing to firms, it is therefore advisable to:

- show that you already know something about the subject of your enquiry;
- explain exactly why you are asking for the information;
- ask specific questions, rather than making a general request for 'information';
- avoid asking for information that would be of value to the firm's competitors – they won't supply it and they will be unimpressed at your naivety in asking for it;
- remember that, in all but the largest firms with their own PR departments, the person who receives your letter will certainly have more urgent things to do than to answer your queries;
- remember that the firm may receive scores of letters similar to yours every week and that it cannot be expected to produce a tailor-made answer to every one of these;
- avoid asking questions that you could have answered by reading published literature;
- keep your letter as brief as possible, ensure that it is legible, and thank the firm in advance for its help.

Interviewing managers and employees

Very much the same points apply when you are interviewing someone employed in a business. In addition, make sure that you keep appointments, don't outstay your welcome, and always write a letter of thanks.

Researching from within a workplace

Having a job or a placement in a company or other organization may offer great opportunities to do research, particularly through participant observation (see p. 14). This is acceptable, provided that you remember and take heed of all the ethical considerations involved and, most importantly, that you gain permission from the head of the organization. If you do anything to annoy or offend the people you are working with, you will not only spoil your own research but you may make it impossible for other students to have placements or jobs at that firm.

ETHICAL GUIDELINES AND ETHICAL COMMITTEES

Ethical guidelines

One way in which researchers have attempted to control unethical methods of investigation has been through the development of ethical guidelines by professional bodies. Many of these, such as the British Sociological Association and the British Psychological Society, have developed professional codes of ethics to assist their members. These alert researchers to their obligations to partici-

▶ Professional codes of ethics often form the basis for the ethical guidelines used by examination bodies for student projects.

pants. The guidelines reflect the values of the profession and cover the problems that frequently occur in a particular profession. However, while there is agreement about proper ethical practice, professional bodies still require that individual researchers develop a personal code of ethics.

Ethical committees

The purpose of an ethical committee is to ensure that any proposed research takes proper account of the ethical issues that arise from the project. An ethical committee can refuse to approve a research proposal if the committee feels that ethical issues are not fully addressed.

Ethical committees are set up by organizations such as the National Health Service, and by colleges, universities and professional bodies. They are normally made up of members of those bodies and researchers. These committees set guidelines that they would expect researchers to follow and research proposals are judged against these guidelines.

Written proposals submitted to ethical committees would normally contain details of the methodology of the project. Proposals should clearly indicate how the researcher plans to deal with issues of confidentiality, privacy and consent and with the publication of results.

Ethical committees are most commonly used in scientific, medical and health-care research because the negative effects of this kind of research can be very harmful. In addition, participants in health and medical research are often patients, who may be especially vulnerable to harm.

Permission from ethical committees

If your research comes under the control of an ethical committee, you will not be able to carry it out until you have submitted a proposal to that committee and it has agreed it. Ethical committees usually provide notes of guidance and forms to be completed by researchers. This can be a very time-consuming process, so if you are working to a tight deadline, you may find it sensible to choose a project that does not require permission from an ethical committee. On the other hand, in the course of gaining permission from an ethical committee a researcher often gains a great deal of advice from the committee.

 Will you need the agreement of an ethical committee?

As a matter of urgency, find out whether the research you are thinking of conducting comes under the control of an ethical committee.

DEVELOPING YOUR OWN CODE OF ETHICS

It is essential that the rights and welfare of those who participate in your project are taken account of at all stages of the research process. This means you must consider the needs of your participants from the very beginning. A personal code of ethics will help you to develop appropriate plans for your particular project.

While there may be agreement about proper ethical practice there is no substitute for a personal code of ethics.

► In any research project, the personal ethics of the researcher is vital to the success of the project.

In adopting a personal code of ethics, each individual researcher assumes responsibility for:

- being aware of all possible ethical issues;
- checking for possible harmful effects on participants;
- being aware of the possible benefits of the project;
- making plans and decisions appropriate to each situation;
- adequately addressing the ethical issues raised by the project;
- upholding important moral values in the project.

 Are there existing ethical codes to follow?

Before you start on your personal code of ethics, ask your tutor whether there are any ethical guidelines published for your field of research. Sometimes these will be provided by your examination board, and sometimes by professional associations such as the British Psychological Society or the British Sociological Association.

Making a start on your own ethical code

You will probably know, at least vaguely, what kind of research project you are going to carry out. A code of ethics is an essential part of your project. It is best to start building your own personal code during your project's planning stages. The following list of questions is designed to guide you in your planning. Using this list you will be able to write your own code of conduct which you can share with your participants and your supervisor. Answer the questions as best you can. Later in this book we shall suggest that you look at the ethical issues in your research again.

1 Selecting your subject
- What kinds of ethical problems does your research subject give rise to? (Look back through this chapter if you are uncertain about what this question means.)
- Which group of people have you chosen to work with? From whom do you need to seek permission to work with them?

► These questions are appropriate where you are researching people. If you are researching businesses, animals, plants or the environment you will need a different kind of code.

- Will you be asking for private information? Could the information that you are seeking cause anxiety or embarrassment?
- Could the results of your project cause pain or distress? If so, to whom?
- What values do you wish to reflect in your project?

2 Selecting your location

If your research is being carried out in more than one location, answer these questions for each location.

- Is it a public or a private setting?
- Are your participants free to choose whether to become involved in your project?
- From whom do you need to seek permission to use this setting? Is there more than one person?
- Will you have personal contact with your participants?
- When will you make contact with your participants?

3 Working with your target group

- How will you make contact with your participants?
- How will you explain your project to your participants?
- Do you need to take account of the age of the participants? If so, how will you do this?
- How will you ensure that your participants understand, as far as possible, about your project?
- How will you maintain the confidentiality of your participants?
- Will you need written or verbal consent? Remember it is difficult to obtain fully informed consent.

4 Collecting your data

- What methodology will you use? What are the ethical problems associated with this method?
- Will your methods of data storage be covered by the Data Protection Act?
- What records will you keep during and after the life of your project?
- Who will have access to these records?
- Will you need to identify your participants? If so, how do you plan to do this?
- How will your results be presented or made public?
- Do you intend to use photographs? If so, how do you plan to reduce identifying features?

5 Publishing your data

- How will you present your data?
- Who has the right to see your report?
- How public will you make your results?
- What are the possible consequences of publication?

► File your answers to these questions. You will refer to them again.

LOOKING AFTER YOURSELF AND COLLEAGUES

Apart from having a responsibility to those whom you research, you also have a responsibility:

- to protect your own physical safety;
- to look after your own reputation;
- not to endanger any colleagues or collaborators who are working with you;
- not to discredit any institution you are attached to;
- not to discredit the kind of research you are conducting.

CHAPTER SUMMARY

This chapter has been about the ethical or moral aspects of conducting research.

- It is important to avoid causing harm to those you research.
- Any risks to those who are researched must be balanced against the benefits to be gained from the results of the research.
- The research you are going to do is unlikely to benefit anyone except yourself, and therefore you should be especially careful to avoid harming others.
- The main ethical considerations in research involving people are:
  - avoiding causing harm to them,
  and, as far as possible,
  - maintaining privacy,
  - maintaining anonymity,
  - maintaining confidentiality,
  - allowing the research participant to exercise informed consent.
- Where research is with businesses, animals, plants or the environment, the importance of avoiding harm and disruption is just as great.
- It is important, and sometimes difficult, to gain permission to research in certain places and/or with certain groups of people.
- There are published codes of ethics for researchers.
- You should devise your own code of ethics for any particular kind of research.
- You must avoid unnecessary risks to yourself and your collaborators, and uphold the reputation of your college and of researchers in general.

In this chapter we asked you to make a first attempt at a code of ethics for your research. Later in the book we shall be asking you to refine this code.

► If you engage in badly designed research that upsets or harms other people, you will also cause trouble for your school or the college you are attached to, and make it difficult for other researchers to do similar research in future.

3 Choosing your topic and developing a title

SOME STARTING TIPS

▶ You may already have been given a subject, or even a title, for your research project or assignment. Nevertheless it will be worthwhile reading through this chapter in order to understand how a piece of research should relate to its title, and vice versa.

As you work through this chapter you will be helped to identify a subject and then to write a provisional title for your project.

Advice from student researchers
When we started writing this chapter we asked some students who were close to completing their research projects what advice they would like to pass on to you – here are some of their comments:

- Plan, plan, plan and then do some more planning.
- Make sure you understand what you are supposed to be doing. If in doubt, ask your lecturer.
- Check what you are being assessed on.
- It's never too early but it can be too late!
- Don't choose too big a topic for your research.
- Choose the title carefully and then keep to it.
- Don't get side-tracked.
- Make sure you can finish the project in the time available.
- Be realistic; don't be too ambitious.
- You don't get any marks for good intentions.
- Choose a project you can afford – even postage or phone calls can be expensive.
- Take advice.

One of the students reminded us of an old saying: 'We learn from our mistakes, but a wise person learns from the mistakes of others.' So we hope that you are wise, and learn from the mistakes and the advice of these students.

SELECTING A SUBJECT AND COMPOSING A TITLE

It is unlikely that you will be given complete freedom to select your project. Usually you will be expected to work within a carefully defined framework provided by your tutor.

There are two essential points about this framework:

1 that you understand what it is and share this understanding with your lecturer;
2 that once you understand the framework, all of your research activity is contained within it.

Can you recognize these points in the advice from the students?

- Make sure that you understand what you are supposed to be doing. If in doubt, ask your lecturer.

- Don't get side-tracked.

Defining your subject and its title is not something you do only at the beginning of the project. You should continually revisit the title throughout the life of the project using the techniques of analysis described later in this chapter.

Let's suppose that a biochemistry student has been given a framework that requires them to investigate enzyme activity. The first title that springs to mind may be:

Investigate the changes that occur when an enzyme is heated.

What further details are needed? Well, what sorts of changes are you going to investigate? What temperature ranges are you dealing with: 20–90°C, or a range running between lower or higher temperatures? By being specific from the outset you won't waste time in, for instance, needlessly testing your enzyme to boiling point.

Let's try a more specific title:

Investigate the rate of enzyme activity as measured by changes in the rate of oxygen production as the temperature of the reaction mixture is varied in the range of 0–70°C.

Even the least scientific of us can see how much more precise this second title is. It says:

- what is to be measured (the rate of enzyme activity);
- how changes are to be measured (in the volume of a gas);
- under what conditions they are to be measured (0–70°C).

The improved title is a condensed version of the research project as a whole, and provides a plan for how the research is to be conducted.

► Composing a title helps in planning a project.

► By 'framework' we mean all the instructions and advice about content and format, the time limits, the length limits and everything else that you have to take into consideration in doing a project.

► Stick to the framework and don't get side-tracked.

► You will probably revise your title several times before you finalize it.

► Good titles for projects are condensed plans of projects.

Revising a title

Compose an improved version of this draft project title:

To find out why some people like rock music more than others and to recommend a marketing strategy for a new rock group.

There are two parts to this title: the finding out part and the recommending part. First, try to work out a better and more specific wording for the finding out part.

In attempting this activity you will probably have realized that the problem with the original title is that it doesn't say how these things are to be found out or who these 'some people' are.

An improved version might be:

An investigation of the musical preferences of a sample of teenagers in Ipswich using personal interviews.

This suggestion indicates:

- the strategy to be used – interviews with a sample;
- the participants in the research – teenagers in Ipswich.

You will probably have used different words in your title. Check to see what information your improved version of the title gave about how the project was to be carried out: how much of a condensed plan was it?

The original title had two halves and it implied that finding out the reasons for musical tastes would in itself lead to recommendations for 'a marketing strategy for a new rock group'. But would this investigation necessarily produce information useful for this purpose?

 Revising the title for market research

Think about the original title again. Would the task of 'finding out' produce information useful for drawing up 'recommendations'. There is a problem here. Try solving it by redrafting the title for the project as a whole.

Our attempt to solve the problem produced this revised title:

An investigation of the musical preferences of a sample of teenage **rock-fans** in Ipswich using personal interviews in order to devise a marketing strategy for a new rock group.

You will see that we have narrowed down the subjects for research to those most likely to support a new rock group. As market researchers we would be wasting our time interviewing lots of people who would never support a rock group. You might think that it would be a good idea to widen the group to be interviewed to include rock fans of any age.

► The improved title indicates the approach to be used: personal interviews with a sample of teenagers. Selecting samples is dealt with in Chapter 6.

You should have seen from this activity that setting titles and planning research are not separate activities. A great deal of planning can be done through setting the title for the research.

► Setting a title is part of planning the project. As you develop your ideas for the project so you will need to modify the title.

Constraints on choosing topics and titles

There are other factors that may hinder or restrict your choice of project or its title. We shall explore these below.

 Learning from the advice of other students

Read again the list of handy hints from the research students (p. 22). Write your own list of between six and eight factors that might restrict you in choosing a project or its title.

Such a list might include: not knowing exactly what is expected of you, not knowing how to start, wanting to know exactly how you will be assessed, not being sure what level you are expected to work to, and not being sure how much detail you would be expected to include, how much it will cost, how long it will take, who will be able to help you, what resources you can use – specialist equipment, libraries or computers – and perhaps whether you are capable of doing the project at all!

► There will also be the ethical problems discussed in Chapter 2.

 Problems in titles

Now that you have identified some of the constraints on choosing your project and its title, perhaps you can identify some problems in the following project titles. Imagine you have been given these titles for a project. For each one write down the problems or questions you would have to answer before starting your research.

1 The effects of a poor diet on children in single-parent families.
2 The benefits of single-sex education.
3 The effect of deforestation on panda populations in China.

In the first title there is an assumption that the children of single-parent families actually have a poor diet. How would you be able to find out whether this is true? Also, what time scale are you using to assess the effects? Six weeks, a year, ten years or half a life time? What size would your sample be? If you only had access to six single-parent families in Cardiff, would your findings be true for all single-parent families in Cardiff, Wales, Europe, the world?

The second title would only allow you to report any benefits you found and not include the disadvantages. Again, what time scale would you use and what benefits are being looked at – benefits to the students, their parents, teaching staff, the government? There is also a problem of access. Is there a single-sex school or college near you? If so, will it cooperate in your research?

The third title, although it seems very interesting, has major problems of access and of time scale. At best you would have to rely on written sources of information and, unless you can read Chinese, that would severely limit the amount of information to which you would have access.

Let us take the first of these three titles and see if we can make a more realistic project from it.

> An investigation into the difficulties of providing an adequate diet for their **pre-school** children **as reported** by **members of the Norwich Gingerbread Group**, using personal interviews and an analysis of the results.

Admittedly this title is longer, but unlike the original it does indicate what is to be done by the researcher. Moreover it indicates a project that looks feasible (or do-able).

▶ Gingerbread Groups are support groups for single-parent families.

▶ There are still some problems with this title. For example, whose definition of an 'adequate diet' are we going to use? What is the relationship between a nutritionist's idea of an 'adequate diet' and the ideas of these single parents? How far could we generalize from our results to other single-parent families? Of course, you can't solve **all** your problems by playing with the title.

 A different title: a different project

Here's another project title in the same general area:

> To investigate the nutrition of a sample of pre-school children drawn from parents attending the Norwich Gingerbread group, over a period of one month, using meal-time diaries completed by each parent.

Compare the two titles and make notes on the way in which the research they propose will differ in method and will differ in what is discovered. Which do you think would be the easier research to conduct and why?

YOUR OWN PROJECT

So far we have been looking at a variety of projects. Now we are going to focus on your project in particular.

 Your first drafts of project titles

Drawing on what you have learned so far, draft at least three titles for your project. Write them on a sheet of paper, with plenty of space between them, and keep them by you as you work through the rest of this chapter. As you read, you will be given plenty of opportunities to revise your titles and to choose between the revised versions.

Project management considerations

By 'project management considerations' we mean all the things you will have to think about in order to decide whether your project is feasible given the time and resources available to you, and whether it is appropriate for the course you are following.

 Your project management considerations

Complete this exercise on A4 sheets of paper and file them carefully as you will need them later when you complete other exercises. You may prefer to jot down the answers to the following questions and then put them into a grid to keep for later.

Question	Example
What discipline is your project?	Sociology
What level?	A level
Is it a 'group project' or is it linked in any way with other projects being undertaken by other students?	No
Is the project linked with other projects conducted by you?	No
Is this the final product?	Yes
When is final hand-in date?	17th May
Other fixed dates?	Proposal 9th Nov. First draft 16th Jan.
Size of project?	15,000 words
Are assessment criteria available?	Yes, printed sheet from tutor
Do you understand all the criteria?	No
Are full instructions available?	Yes
Is the project to be word-processed?	Yes
Are instructions available covering the presentation?	No
Do you know how to interpret your results?	No
Do you have to use specific methodologies?	No
Will you need specialist equipment?	No
Can you estimate the cost?	No
Who is going to pay?	Me
What happens to the project ?	Don't know
Do you need to get permission from anyone?	No

► You may not be able to answer all these questions now. But you should know the answers before you begin serious work on your project. The rest of the chapter should help you with this.

The importance of making neat notes

Do take the time and effort to write up the results of this exercise as neatly as possible. It is all too easy to scribble, only to find that your notes are illegible when you come back to them at a later date. One of the authors of this book remembers writing up pages of notes from a library book but being unable to read half of them when she needed to use those notes in her assignment. She had to re-order the book from the library, wait three weeks for it as it was being used by another library user and then do the work all over again. So keep neat notes and file them carefully.

We hope that the activity above has helped you to focus more clearly on your project. What you have written should give you the basic structure for the management of your project. It is often easy to overlook some of these initial management points in your haste to get on with the project itself, but it is important to be clear about the required structure before selecting your project or its title.

Let us now examine some of the problems that might have come up in doing the activity.

Multidiscipline problems

One of the difficulties that you may have found is that your proposed project doesn't fall within the bounds of a single discipline. For example, suppose you were going to undertake a project studying the effects of cancer on patients. Here you might need to include medical, psychological and even economic research as part of your investigation.

▶ How to choose research methods, and how different disciplines relate to and demand different methodologies is dealt with in Chapters 4, 5 and 6.

Identifying the disciplines of your proposed project will help you to decide whether you may be in danger of taking on too much. Some disciplines and their research methodologies are very demanding in terms of time, resources, skills and cost.

The earlier example of investigating the effects of cancer might require three separate research projects, each demanding appropriate time and skills. The medical aspect would cover the physiology and treatment of the disease, the psychological research could cover the manner in which the patient reacts to the disease and how this influences the patient's interaction with others, and the economic research could cover how the patient and their family cope with increased expenses, perhaps on a reduced income, during the management of the disease, and maybe the financial and social costs of treating the disease.

▶ You can use a title to limit the disciplines you are going to work in. For example: 'An investigation into the psychological effects. . . ' This choice must be consistent with the criteria for assessment.

It is clear that many proposed projects contain more than one discipline. You might like to see if you can identify which discipline our earlier rock music project would be based on.

> An investigation of the musical preferences of a sample of teenage rock-fans in Ipswich using personal interviews in order to devise a marketing strategy for a new rock group.

For the first part of this title you are simply asking people their opinions. Opinion research of this kind is a largely statistical activity, although you would need some psychological know-how for conducting the interviews. The second part of the title demands marketing theory, which is itself a hybrid of sociology, psychology and economics. However, there are few multidiscipline problems lurking in this title. Now change the title just a little to read:

An investigation of the **reasons for** the musical preferences of a sample of teenage rock-fans in Ipswich using personal interviews.

This is now a much larger piece of work. We are attempting to find out not only what musical preferences these people have but also why they have them.

 How many subject disciplines are involved?

Make a list of factors that influence your own musical preferences and identify which discipline areas might help in explaining them.

You may have included some or all of these:

Contributory factors	Discipline
Influences from childhood experiences	Psychology and Sociology
Membership of social groups	Social Psychology
Related to the calming or stimulating effects of music	Psychology
Related to the ability to purchase tapes or CDs or to attend concerts or buy musical instruments	Economics
Related to the way we hear or don't hear sounds and how we vocalize.	Physics and Biology
Associated with the rhythm and tonal quality of sacred music	Religion
Related to the way particular musical trends are marketed and made available to sections of the public	Business Studies

We hope this section has demonstrated that a few minutes at the beginning of your project spent thinking about the discipline(s) involved will allow you to plan much more successfully.

 Indicating the discipline in the title

Take the three provisional titles you drafted earlier. Can you revise them to indicate the disciplines that will be involved in your project? For example, could you write: 'A sociological investigation into. . .', or 'A psychological approach to. . .' or even 'A psychosocial investigation into. . .'? If you feel inclined to write: 'A multidisciplinary investigation into. . .', then think very carefully. Multidisciplinary projects are usually very big projects, or, if they are small, they do not do justice to any of the disciplines involved.

▶ Of course you don't *have* to write the discipline into the title. The important thing is to know what discipline you are working within.

Working to the right level

The level your project will have to reach will depend primarily on

▶ One of the best ways of gaining an idea of the level required is to look at work produced by past students.

what course you are following. Is it a GCSE course, an A level project, a GNVQ assignment or an undergraduate project? All of these courses, and others, have clearly defined aims and objectives that are usually provided with the syllabus. Your tutor will normally help you to ensure that you meet all of these aims and objectives. This will be done by providing clear goals and learning outcomes for each assignment that is set.

In some circumstances it may be helpful for you to use these objectives as a check list to make sure that your project meets all the requirements.

Earlier in this chapter, we emphasized how important it is to define the framework of the project. Here again are the two important points about the framework of the project:

1 that you understand what the framework is and share that understanding with your tutor;
2 that once you understand the framework, all of your research activity is contained within it.

Specified objectives, learning outcomes and performance criteria are three ways that you measure the required level and it is essential that you check regularly with your tutor that your level is right. This can be done either by presenting an initial project outline, through formal and informal discussions or tutorials with your tutor, or by reporting interim findings and conclusions.

Often you will be helped in achieving the right level by your choice of reading material for the project. If you are undertaking a GCSE project you don't have to restrict yourself to GCSE books only, but you must make sure that the material from more advanced books is entirely relevant to your project and that you thoroughly understand it.

▶ For more about using the library, see Chapter 8.

Also remember that one of the factors that will determine the level will be the time allocated to undertake the project. This may seem very obvious, but if you have four weeks to undertake a project and you have completed it in one week, it is unlikely to be to the level required. Similarly, if you have been allocated 3,000 words to write up your project and your introduction alone takes 2,000 words, it is unlikely that you are working to the right level.

Links between your project and others

Your project may be linked to other projects being undertaken by other students. If your project is a small part of a major project, this may limit what you are able to do. In these circumstances it is essential that you, and everyone else involved, know what contribution you are making to the major project. Team planning should be the approach here.

Alternatively, it may be that your current project is linked to other projects that you have already conducted, or will be expected to undertake later. If so, when you plan your project, you will have to take the others into consideration.

Final projects

If this project is the final piece of research in your current course of study it will probably carry the greatest weighting for assessment. It will almost certainly be the most demanding piece of work you undertake for the course. You may have to use the project to show what you have learned from lectures and tutorials and how you have applied this in doing research. Your tutor may tell you what concepts and knowledge you should apply in the project, or it may be part of the assessment to show that you can apply relevant knowledge and concepts without assistance from a tutor.

Group projects

If this is a project carried out by a group of students then very careful planning will be necessary. You will need to:

- select and agree the title and the plan together;
- decide who is going to do what and by when;
- have frequent meetings to review your progress and revise your plans;
- develop mechanisms to resolve differences.

You will also need to look at the assessment specifications to decide how you are going to show who did what in the final report.

Assessment criteria and project titles

You will only arrive at a suitable title if you make use of the available assessment criteria for the project.

 Checking the assessment criteria

Obtain a copy of the assessment criteria for your project. Read all the criteria and make sure you understand them all. Keep a copy of the criteria carefully filed.

If you are in any doubt about the assessment criteria, ask your teacher or lecturer. Remember that you can't get good marks, or possibly any marks at all, if you don't understand how marks are awarded and for what.

GNVQ core skills

If you are taking a GNVQ then your research assignment may provide evidence for the assessment of your core skills. The most important core skills in this context are: Communication, Application of Number, and Information Technology.

You may be able to design your assignment to make sure that it produces the core skill evidence required. The GNVQ specifications change from time to time and you should ask your tutor for a copy

▶ It is worth asking teaching staff what criteria they use when they assess projects. Are they assessing your ability to do research? Or assessing your knowledge and how much you have learned from lectures?

▶ Group projects, particularly GNVQ assignments, often carry additional assessment specifications which reward individuals for their ability to work in a team.

▶ The assessment criteria may contain 'command words' such as 'analyse' or 'evaluate'. These terms are explained later in the chapter.

of the current specifications. Photocopy these, or copy them out, and put a tick wherever your project seems likely to produce evidence that meets the performance criteria. Identify any skills that are not covered in your assignment and see if you can find a way to include them.

Resources and project titles

When you draft a project title, you are at the same time making a resource statement. You will be identifying the resources you will need by your choice of words in the title. For example, if the title includes 'personal interviews' and 'with a sample of 25...' then you probably have allocated at least 15 hours for conducting the interviews themselves, before taking into consideration the time taken to get you face to face with an interviewee.

 Resource listing

Take your three draft titles, and for each make a list of the resources, apart from time, which the research would require. Include any resources you will have to create yourself such as questionnaires or letters to gain permission to conduct research. Where you will have to pay the bills, estimate the cost of the resources. Don't forget the resources you will need to produce the final report, such as word-processing facilities. File these lists.

 Project management and your titles

Take your three titles from p. 26, your notes on project management considerations, the assessment criteria for the project and your list of resources. Look carefully at each title and decide which titles indicate projects that:

- would meet the requirements given to you by your tutor;
- would meet the assessment criteria;
- are feasible, given the time and resources available to you.

Delete any titles that now look inappropriate or impossible and if this leaves you with no titles at all, draft some more and repeat the activity.

► Find out if there is a possibility for extending any deadline dates and whether any marks are deducted for late submissions.

► At this stage you will probably want to discuss your titles with a tutor to gain further advice.

COMMAND WORDS

The instructions you are given for projects, the printed assessment criteria by which your project is to be assessed, and your project titles themselves will contain 'command words', such as 'describe' or 'analyse' or 'evaluate'. These have two purposes. First, they tell the reader (including the assessor) what it is that you propose to do.

The reader can then decide whether you have actually done what the command words have indicated. Second, by including certain command words in your title you can be clear about what it is that you have to do, you can attempt to do it, and finally, you can check that you have done it.

Defining command words

To make sure you understand some of the most common command words, write down your own definitions for the following command words, and then check the definitions in a dictionary, such as the *Collins Concise English Dictionary*. After you have completed this activity we shall give you some more advice on these words.

Analyse	Measure
Assess	Outline
Compare and contrast	Relate
Criticize	State
Define	Summarize
Describe	Trace
Evaluate	

Checking the assessment criteria for command words

The text that follows explains the meaning of particular command words. As you read, identify where these words occur in the assessment criteria (or other instructions) for your own project. Use the above grid, or a copy of it, to make your own notes.

Common command words

'Define' and 'state'

These types of command words are prescriptive. If you do not do what is asked of you, you will probably lose marks. In order to 'define' or 'state' you will normally need to collect the information from, for example, a text book, and then either quote it verbatim or define it in your own words.

Remember that there may be a variety of interpretations of some factual material and you may need to obtain information from more than one source.

Using the earlier example about the diet of children in single-parent families you might be asked to **state** the main components of a balanced diet. At one level everyone with a basic knowledge would define this as: water, fibre, carbohydrate, proteins, lipids, vitamins and minerals. At a more advanced level many of those general terms would be sub-divided and quantified, thus giving more precise information about nutritional requirements. In this

▶ **Prescriptive** means giving directions or rules.

▶ Be careful with the word 'define'. A definition taken from elsewhere won't always be acceptable; sometimes you will have to devise the definition yourself – see Chapter 5.

▶ Chapter 11 gives you advice on quoting references and avoiding plagiarism.

case you would outline the different perspectives of, for instance, organizations such as the World Health Organization, and various governments, each of which may recommend different amounts. You will see that the meaning of 'define' and 'state', depends on the level of your project.

'Summarize'

▶ An **outline** is a kind of summary.

The words 'summarize' and 'outline' require you to do more than simply repeat what you have read or measured. You have to make some judgements about your information. With this type of command word the actions that you need to take should be clear, but once again it is essential that you carry them out as instructed or you will lose marks in the assessment.

▶ The requirement to be 'clear and concise' is important in all aspects of research and its presentation. You will not get more marks simply for writing more words. Marks will always be given where your ideas and arguments are expressed clearly and in a way that is simple for the reader to understand.

The *Collins Concise English Dictionary* defines 'summarize' as 'express concisely' and defines 'concise' as 'brief and to the point'. To express something briefly and to the point, you have to select the main points and reject the minor details. Your ability to do this will demonstrate that you understand the material. Remember, you will need to be able to explain the reasons for your selection and rejection decisions.

'Compare and contrast'

These words ask you to identify both similarities and differences. You may be required only to list similarities and differences – lists like this are a very good way of dealing with contrasts. However, as the research becomes more detailed, it is likely that you will also have to analyse some of these similarities and differences.

At one extreme the contrast will reflect things that are entirely opposite to one another. However you will soon find that research gives very few absolute contrasts. It is often necessary to use statistical techniques to determine whether things can truly be said to be different or the same.

'Analyse'

The dictionary defines this as: 'break down into components or essential features', which is exactly what you should do.

Go back to the work you did earlier in the chapter (p. 24), when you were thinking about what a project title might mean. To refresh your memory, here are three titles that were used as examples:

1 To find out why some people like rock music more than others
2 An investigation of the musical preferences of a sample of teenage rock-fans in Ipswich using personal interviews
3 An investigation of the **reasons for** the musical preferences of a sample of teenage rock-fans in Ipswich using personal interviews

▶ Analysis always involves breaking down into parts.

We are going to analyse these titles in terms of the feasibility of the projects they propose.

Methods	Subjects	Aims
Title 1	Vague title (unclear what is to be done)	Unclear whois to be studied	Vague
Title 2	Precise title (indicates what should be done)	Sample of teenagers from Ipswich	Discover musical preferences
Title 3	Precise title (indicates what is to be done)	Sample of teenage rock-fans	Discover musical preferences and reasons for them

You can see from this that the first title is not a workable title for a project. The second two titles do indicate feasible projects, in principle, but the third is much more wide-ranging and ambitious than the second.

So what analysis have we done? We have chosen three points of comparison – methods, subjects and aims – and we have compared the three titles according to these. Note that we have done the analysis for a particular purpose: that of identifying a feasible project. We could have analysed the same titles for other reasons, and then we might have chosen different points of comparison. Analysing doesn't necessarily mean drawing up grids and filling in boxes, but this is often helpful.

► **Comparing and contrasting** involves **analysing**. **Summarizing** means that you analyse and decide what is more and what is less important in order to decide what to keep in and what to leave out.

 Analysing your own titles for feasibility

Now analyse your own titles from p. 26 with a view to deciding which is the most feasible. You may wish to add other criteria such as 'cost' and 'time'.

'Evaluate'

In order to evaluate something you must first analyse it to identify the key points.

The term 'evaluate' implies making a judgement that something is more valuable than something else. You will probably meet the term 'evaluate' in the following circumstances:

► To **criticize** and to **assess** usually mean the same as to **evaluate**.

1 You are asked to evaluate data (or evidence, or techniques of research) to reach a conclusion as to which gave the more convincing results: for example, 'Evaluate interviews and questionnaires as ways of investigating opinions about. . . '
2 You are asked to evaluate your own project. This is a common requirement of student project work and an important aspect of grading in GNVQ. Here you are being asked to give an objective account of how well you think you conducted your research, what its strengths and weaknesses are, what you learned from doing it and perhaps what you might do differently on a future occasion. The comparing and the contrasting here is between what you actually achieved and your speculations about how things might have been better or worse.
3 You are asked to evaluate some policy or practice: for example, 'Evaluate the local authority programme for

► Assessment of a project is a process of evaluation, and the assessment specifications are the criteria against which your project will be evaluated.

delivering care in the community.' In this case you would be setting up criteria (or standards of judgement), and then comparing the performance of the local authority against them.

Command words and levels of work

The use of command words gives an indication of the level of work expected from you. More marks are usually given for the higher order skills of analysing, assessing and evaluating.

Lower skill levels	**Higher skill levels**
Define	Analyse
Describe	Criticize
Measure	Assess
State	Evaluate

▶ To measure is to define in numbers.

The command words may also indicate what is more and what is less important for assessment. For example, you might be asked to 'Describe . . . and then analyse'. Here it is likely that most of the marks will be given for the analysis. But if you are asked only to 'Define', then there are unlikely to be many marks for analysis.

 Marks for command words

Look again at the assessment specifications for your course and your project. These may indicate how marks are weighted for, say, describing as against, say, analysing and evaluating. If they do not, then ask your tutor whether your project should be basically a descriptive, defining, measuring, stating kind of project, or whether it should be an analysing and evaluating kind of project. Use this information to plan your project.

> ### Originality
> It is easy to be misled by the term 'original'. The kind of project you, as a student, are going to do isn't going to produce anything remarkably original. What 'original' means in this context is that the project is your own work (or the work of the project team) and not something copied from books, or from one of last year's students. Be creative, but don't be so creative as to depart from the framework you have been given to work within.

▶ See Chapter 11 on plagiarism.

ETHICAL CONSIDERATIONS AND PERMISSIONS

In Chapter 2 you read about the ethical considerations for projects. Now is the time to double-check your project proposal for ethics.

Checking the ethics of your proposal

Take your project titles and look back to pp. 19–20 of Chapter 2 where there is a list of questions for identifying the ethical problems posed by projects. Use the checklist with each of your titles. Delete or amend any titles posing ethical problems that are impossible to solve.

 Predicting permissions

For each of your project titles write a list of the people or agencies from whom you will need to obtain permission to conduct research. Where it looks likely that you will not be able to obtain the necessary permission, or at least not in the time available, delete or amend the title.

DECIDING ON A TITLE

By now you should have one or more project titles that seem:

- understandable, because you know what it would mean to follow the commands in the title;
- feasible, given the resources available to you in terms of money, equipment, cooperation from others and so on;
- appropriate for the level of work required, the kinds of topics permitted and the methods of research allowed.

 A final check and a first choice

Check your project titles against the list above. Which one seems to be the most understandable, feasible and appropriate? Ask advice from a tutor if necessary. This is the project title that you should start with. If you are not happy with any of your proposals then use the relevant sections of this chapter to draft and evaluate some more.

Research is dynamic

Remember, research is dynamic. As you undertake the planning and the research itself, your project may change. This is a normal part of any kind of research and you will have to go on asking the following questions:

1 Will the changed project still meet the criteria necessary to pass and to be successful?
2 Do I have to negotiate a change in the proposed project with my tutor? If so, what are the procedures for this?
3 At what stage will no further changes be possible?

The kind of thinking you have been doing in this chapter should be applied at all stages of your research project.

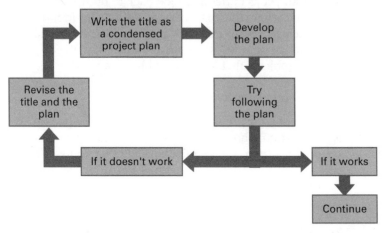

Figure 3.1 Flowchart showing the process of devising a project plan and title

Although this chapter comes early in the book, you will need to do the kinds of things it suggests again and again. Remember the advice you received at the beginning of the chapter:

Plan, plan, plan and then do some more planning.

 Avoiding problems in advance

Turn to the last chapter of the book, which is titled: 'What to do when things go wrong'. Scan quickly through it. These are the kinds of problem that can often be avoided by careful planning in advance.

CHAPTER SUMMARY

This chapter has been about planning your research project through drafting and redrafting project titles. We have drawn attention to the importance of:

- writing titles as condensed project plans;
- writing titles and planning projects that are feasible in terms of the resources available to you and the cooperation you are likely to get from others;
- writing titles and planning projects that will meet the requirements for assessment;
- writing titles and planning projects that are ethically acceptable.

We have also warned you that planning isn't just something you will do at the beginning of a project, but that planning and replanning will continue to the end.

Choosing your method

Chapter objectives

After working through this chapter you will be able to:

▌ list a range of methodologies;

▌ recognize which methodologies are suited to which purposes;

▌ formulate hypotheses for different research titles and at different levels;

▌ take account of factors constraining the selection of different methodologies;

▌ make a preliminary choice of the kind of methodology you will be using in your project.

ASKING THE RIGHT QUESTIONS

Research is about asking questions, such as:

- Why do you like rock music?
- How many people will buy a new type of chocolate bar?
- What happens to a rate of reaction if we heat enzymes?
- What will be the impact of a new housing development on the local economy?
- What kinds of people use the local leisure centre?

After we have asked the questions, we have to find a way for them to be answered.

We hope that by now you have at least established a provisional title for your project. The next task is to decide exactly what questions you should ask.

▶ Effective research means asking the right questions.

> The questions you intend to answer through your research will influence your choice of methodology.

'Descriptive' and 'theory-testing' research

Sometimes the question for research is very broad and very vague, such as:

> What's going on around here?

If you think about it, one always has to ask this type of broad question before more precise questions can be asked. Answering such

▶ Because **descriptive** research is often the first stage in a research process it is sometimes called 'exploratory research'. However, your project might begin with **exploratory** research and end with a plan for further research that you may never carry out.

broad questions involves what is often called 'descriptive research' or 'exploratory research'. Descriptive research, particularly in the social sciences, is often the first phase of a research project. Think of the process as a series of stages, where stages 1 and 2 are largely descriptive, stages 3 and 4 are explanatory, and stage 4 involves framing a hypothesis to test an explanation.

1 What's going on around here? (And what's the best way of finding out and describing it?)

> How do drivers behave at pedestrian crossings?
> (Consider different kinds of drivers, different kinds of crossings, different kinds of pedestrians, different times of day, different states of traffic flow. Observe to find out.)

2 What's particularly interesting about what's going on around here? (And what's the best way of finding out and describing this?)

> It is beginning to look as though male drivers behave differently from female drivers and maybe each behave differently towards different kinds of pedestrians. Make more focused observations.

3 What explanations can be given for particularly interesting observations? What theories could we use to do the explaining?

> There are theories about the differences between male and female behaviour. I need to read up on these.

4 What questions do we need to ask in order to test the explanation given by the theory; what hypotheses should we frame and how should we test them?

▶ On framing hypotheses, see later in the chapter (p. 43).

You should see from the above that at least the early stages of research often involve finding out what it is happening that is worth further investigation.

 Is your project exploratory and descriptive, or explanatory and theory-testing?

> Look at your proposed project title. Which of the stages above does it require you to cover? If it is allowed by the assessment specifications then your research might start at 1 and stop at 2. Or it might run from 1 to 3 or 1 to 4. Or alternatively you may have been given an explanation or theory to test, in which case stages 1 and 2 will be taken for granted, and your project will focus on 3 and 4. You will probably be focusing on stages 3 and 4 if your project is in the 'hard sciences' such as biology, chemistry or physics. If you are completing an assignment for a GNVQ course, your research will often be descriptive, perhaps making comparisons between two examples.

'Pure' and 'applied' research

Some kinds of project will be dedicated entirely to finding things out. Others will involve either applying what is found out or making recommendations for action.

For example:

> An investigation into the likely effects on student recruitment of increasing crèche provision at the college – to be conducted using questionnaires with a sample of mature students which, when analysed, will form the basis for recommendations to the college governors.

You will see that in this example the 'right questions' will all be about 'what if there were more crèche places?' This is not the kind of research that tests academic theories. It is the kind of research that produces information that will be useful for decision-making. This will influence the kinds of questions asked, and the kinds of methods used to get the answers.

 Pure or applied?

Look at your proposed project title. Does it suggest a piece of applied research designed to produce information for decision-making? Or does it suggest a piece of pure research designed to produce academically interesting knowledge? Your project could, of course, do both, but if so you may be taking on too much.

Prioritizing your aims

You will have limited time and limited resources for your project and you will probably be in a position where you can do one, but only one, of the following:

• a good piece of exploratory and descriptive research;
• a good piece of explanatory and theory-testing research;
• a good piece of applied research resulting in well-founded recommendations.

Different kinds of research: different kinds of research question

Exploratory and descriptive research

Exploratory and descriptive research starts from questions about what is happening, designed so that you can give an adequate description: questions of who, what, when, how much and how many.

Explanatory and theory-testing research

Explanatory and theory-testing research starts from questions

---

► Another kind of applied research is **evaluation research**, where you use research techniques to decide whether some organization is or is not achieving what it should be achieving. Evaluation research usually ends with **recommendations** for improved performance.

asking how far what is observed supports or undermines a particular explanation, usually framed as a hypothesis.

Applied research

Applied research starts from questions designed to produce information on which future decisions can be based: questions about how well things are being done (evaluation) or questions designed to establish what would be the consequences of new or changed policies.

 Your research questions

Using your project title, list the questions that need to be answered to complete the research project. When you have prepared your list of questions you will be aware that some questions are much larger than others. There may be some that either cannot be answered fully or cannot be answered at all by the project you propose.

▶ If you discover that your project isn't going to answer your questions, then *either* change your project plans *or* change the questions. See Chapter 3.

▶ At this early stage you will probably be unclear about your response to the questions in the box. You may need to come back to them later.

A checklist for your research questions

- Are the research questions appropriate for your project, being *one* of the following:
     exploratory and descriptive ☐
     explanatory and theory testing ☐
     applied and designed to produce
     recommendations? ☐
- When the questions are answered will your work meet the criteria set for your particular project? ☐
- Can you answer the questions within the time and the resources available for your project? ☐
- When you have answered the questions will you have achieved what your project title set out to do? ☐
- Will the answers to the questions be meaningful to other people involved in this area? ☐
- Do you have the skills necessary to do the research to answer the questions, or do you need to learn them? ☐

We hope that you now realize how important it is to identify the right questions at this planning stage of your research project. It is at the planning stage that you are most able to make any amendments that might be necessary. It can become a real disaster if you are three-quarters of the way through your project and you realize that you haven't been asking the right questions.

Do you remember that first piece of advice from the research students in chapter one?

'Plan, plan, plan and then do some more planning.'

HYPOTHESES

For much research, rather than asking questions, we make statements that can then be tested. These carefully defined statements are often referred to as hypotheses (in the plural) or a hypothesis (in the singular).

This kind of research process can therefore be referred to as 'hypothesis testing'. Researchers will often set out with the intention of proving or disproving a particular hypothesis by testing it.

> ### A hypothesis
> A hypothesis is an 'if–then' statement: **if** this explanation is correct **then** this should happen, or be true, or be observable, or whatever. For example:
>
> > **If** swallows migrate south in response to shortening day-length **then** their leaving date each year should correlate with the amount of time between sun-up and sun-down and the amount of cloud cover.
>
> Or
>
> > **If** swallows migrate south in response to falling temperature **then** their leaving date each year should correlate with temperature measurements.

You will see that each hypothesis is a way of testing a particular explanation: **if** such and such is true, **then** it is possible that this suggested explanation is true.

Writing a hypothesis

The box above gives you two examples of what are often called **experimental hypotheses** (whether or not an actual experiment is going on). You may be required to use an alternative called a **null hypothesis**. For our swallows this might be:

> There will be no (statistically significant) relationship between day-length and the leaving date of swallows.

This back-to-front way of framing hypotheses is preferred in science because it is conventionally accepted that it is impossible ever to prove the truth of an explanation. Thus even if there were a correlation between day-length and the migration of swallows, this would not prove that changes in day-length determined the date of leaving; all kinds of other things might be doing this. By contrast, it is much easier to *disprove* an explanation. If the null hypothesis is found to be true, then day-length can't be the explanation. If the null hypothesis turns out to be untrue, then the day-length explanation would remain a possibility.

► If your research is not explanatory and theory-testing, then you could skip this section. But we suggest you read through it all the same.

► **Correlation** means that one thing varies in association with another. Tides, for example, are correlated with phases of the moon.

► 'Statistically significant' is included because statistical methods are often used to test hypotheses.

▶ The chi-square test is a statistical test used to compare the goodness of fit of theoretical and observed frequency distributions.

Like project titles, the best hypotheses are those that are condensed plans for action. We can do better than the examples above in this respect. For the null hypothesis we could write:

> There will be no statistically significant correlation as judged using a chi-square test between day-length as measured by the time between sun-up and sun-down and the leaving date of 50 per cent of swallows from the roosting area adjacent to the Church in Woodbridge.

You will see that as you make your hypothesis more precise you have to think carefully about definitions (of relationship, of day-length, of leaving); about methods used to collect information and about interpreting the results (is disappearing from a roost site the same as 'migrating'?).

 Your own hypotheses

> If your project involves formulating hypotheses, then try your hand at formulating both a hypothesis and a null hypothesis for your project.

▶ Time spent at the formulation stage is usually time saved later.

Spending time on formulating your hypotheses

If you are testing hypotheses then you will need to invest a great deal of time in getting the formulation of the hypotheses right. Ask your colleagues to try tearing your hypotheses to pieces, and then reformulate to meet their objections and ask them to do it again. Always ask your tutor's advice before finalizing a hypothesis unless you are required to formulate it without tutorial help.

METHODOLOGY

In Chapter 5 some common research methodologies will be explored, but in this chapter we would like to use your experience at undertaking investigations in the past to help you to understand what is important about particular methods.

Experimental method

Most students will have undertaken a simple experimental investigation in their early studies, whether it was into the composition of a food stuff, the effect of light on photosynthesis in green plants, or the effect of magnets on iron filings. We shall deal with just one of these examples of a scientific investigation to demonstrate some of the key features of experimental research.

Below we have set out the stages of a simple scientific investigation that you may have done at school. You will see that the stages of the experiment are set out on the left of the grid, and on the right of the grid we have made comments about the role of the various stages or points in the process as a whole.

Comments

Title:
To investigate the effect of light on the process of photosynthesis in a green plant

Note that this title is quite broad, although it does indicate a variable, which is light. It also specifies the subject of our investigation, which will be a green plant. Using the previous section you might like to make the title more precise and to write a hypothesis or a null hypothesis.

► A **variable** is something that varies – usually something important.

Apparatus:
Geranium plant; de-starched paper; Maltese crosses; paper clips; boiling water bath; 70% alcohol; iodine solution; white tile; forceps; clock

The apparatus listed is very simple both in terms of its cost and availability, and in the skills required to use it. In order to arrive at this list of apparatus, a resource survey has been undertaken, and initial decisions have been made about the time and skills necessary to complete the experiment. This is also an important planning procedure for determining any safety issues – here the key word will be 'boiling'.

Method:
1 Using the paper clips, fix the Maltese crosses to some of the leaves of the geranium plant. The leaves with the crosses will be referred to as the 'test' leaves. Leaves without crosses will be referred to as the 'control' leaves.
2 De-starch the geranium plant by placing it in a dark cupboard for 24 hours.
3 Place the plant in bright sunlight for 3 days.
4 Take samples of test and control leaves, taking care to keep each group identifiable.
5 Place each group of leaves into boiling water for 1 minute and then transfer them immediately to warm 70% alcohol.
6 Leave each leaf in the warm alcohol for 1 minute or until no further green colour remains in the leaf.

This type of scientific method is written clearly and concisely so that it can be repeated exactly by another researcher. This is important in this type of research because it allows other experimenters to check whether the results are repeatable and therefore reliable. That is, they can trust what you have done. Reliability is important in all research, as it is possible that you did the experiment entirely incorrectly, yet are now claiming that your results are correct. In addition, throughout the history of science there have been several well-known cases in which experimenters have actually cheated and claimed results that they were never able to achieve.

► In experiments the 'experimental/test' group is the one that is experimented on. The 'control' group is the one against which the experimental group is compared.

► Safety precautions should be taken to avoid contact with boiling water and to ensure that the alcohol is not set on fire.

► Iodine turns starch black and is an **indicator** of starch.

7 Remove the leaves. Place them flat on a white tile and flood with the iodine solution. Note the presence of black staining and any patterns appearing on the leaf.

8 Compare the test and control leaves.

9 Record the results by means of diagrams.

Control of variables in experiments

The key to understanding experimental method is the idea of **control**. The example starts from the knowledge that photosynthesis produces starch, but many things apart from light might produce starch in leaves, so the experimental method is an attempt to screen out the effects of anything other than light. This is done mainly by having an experimental group of leaves and a control group of leaves. All the leaves are treated identically, except for excluding light from the experimental or 'test' leaves. You may have noticed that the leaves were all taken from the same plant, which is another way of ensuring that they are similar in all respects apart from exposure to light.

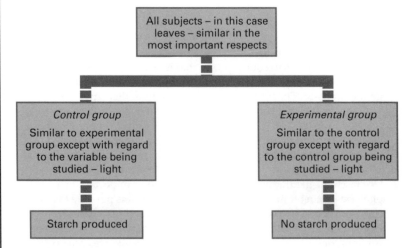

Figure 4.1 Experimental method used to show the effect of light on photosynthesis

You can see that, with this experimental setup, it seems highly probable that the differences in starch production were due to the differences in exposure to light (and nothing else), since this was the only way in which the two groups of leaves differed from each other.

Different kinds of variable

Dependent variables

In this experiment the **dependent variable** was the amount of starch produced.

► **DV** – dependent variable; **IV** – independent variable.

It is called the 'dependent variable' because it is dependent on something else: in this case the assumption is that the dependent variable – starch production – is caused by the independent variable – light exposure.

Independent variables

In this experiment the **independent variable** being studied was the amount of light to which the leaves were exposed. It is called the independent variable because it is assumed to be part of the cause of the dependent variable. There are lots of other independent variables around, such as the cell structure of the leaf and the temperature of the air, but in this experiment they have all been standardized so that the control group and the experimental group are the same with regard to these variables. While these are held constant, the independent variable is manipulated by the researcher and the effects on the dependent variable are studied.

It is important to understand that we can decide which variables are dependent and which are independent according to our research interest. For example, the evolution of plant species and the big bang at the beginning of the universe are among the many causes of photosynthesis, but we don't call them 'independent variables' here because we aren't interested in them for this particular experiment.

Intervening variables

Intervening variables come in between; they intervene between the independent and the dependent variable. Since the process of photosynthesis is very complicated, all the chemicals involved at all the stages of photosynthesis intervene between the cause (the light) and the effect (starch production). For this experiment we are not interested in them: we have 'black-boxed' the process of photosynthesis (i.e. we have excluded it from our attention) and we are simply looking at an input (light) and an output (starch).

Confounding variables

Confounding variables are all those variables we should have controlled but failed to. They will confound, or muddy, the outcome of the research, and possibly invalidate it completely. In the experiment described, there are unlikely to be any significant confounding variables, but in research with human participants it is very difficult to exclude the confounding variables that arise in particular from the fact that people know they are the subjects of experiments or research. The use of 'placebos' is one way researchers have tried to deal with this problem.

> ► You could also say that the DV was the colour of the iodine because this was what was actually observed.

> ► Inert substances administered as medicines but having no pharmacological effects are called **placebos**.

The placebo effect: a confounding variable

Before it was recognized, the placebo effect must have been a very important confounding variable in medical research. The placebo effect refers to the fact that many people feel better, and some actually get better, just by taking a pill, even when the pill is made of an inert substance that can't affect their physiology directly. The placebo effect means that if an experimental group is given a pill, and the control group is given no pill, then some of the difference between the two groups will be due to being given a pill (any pill), and not to the pharmacological effect of this particular pill as such. Today it is usual practice to give the control group a placebo pill – usually a vitamin C tablet – to control this confounding variable. If *both* groups are given a pill, then the differences between them are most likely to be due to the biochemical effects of the kind of pill given to the experimental group.

Experiments with people

In psychology, in medical research, and occasionally in education, experiments are conducted with people as the subjects. However, there are several constraints on using experimental methods with people, and care must be taken in interpreting the results.

Ethical problems

Many experiments that might be done with people are ruled out for ethical reasons. It would obviously be unethical to do an experiment that significantly affected someone's future, especially if it made the future worse.

Apart from the possibility of doing harm, experiments with people raise ethical issues about lies and deceit. To be successful, many experiments with people require the experimenter to mislead the participants as to the purpose of the research, or at least to withhold information from them about whether they had been chosen for the experimental or the control group. Some researchers are unwilling to treat their participants in this way.

Practical problems

There are some areas of research where it would not only be unethical, but also impractical, to use an experimental method with people. For example, someone interested in the effects of childhood experience on later life could hardly select experimental and control groups of children at birth and control the way they were brought up. Similarly a researcher interested in the operation of the stock-exchange would never be able to gain the cooperation of stock market traders and get them to buy and sell in one way one day, and buy and sell in another on another day. Where experiments are ruled out for practical reasons, researchers may look for 'natural experiments' to study.

Natural experiments or comparative method
The laboratory researcher has a good chance of arranging things so that he or she can control variables and make them

▶ In medical research, experiments that are potentially harmful to the participants are sometimes performed. There is an example on pp. 5–6 of Chapter 2.

come up in particular combinations: for example, leaves with and leaves without exposure to light. In the social sciences this is rarely possible, so instead researchers look out for naturally occurring situations where the variables they are interested in interact in the ways they are interested in. For example, a researcher interested in the effects of mixed-ability teaching in maths might look out for situations where maths was taught to mixed-ability groups, and make comparisons with other naturally occurring situations where maths was taught to classes streamed by measured ability. However, it is rarely the case that the groups studied differ only in the variables of interest, so there are many opportunities for confounding variables to become involved.

Astronomers, meteorologists, oceanographers, ecologists and other scientists who can't set up artificial situations for research also look for natural experiments to study.

CONTROL VERSUS NATURALISM

One of the main strengths of experimental research is that it allows the researcher to control the research situation. Put another way, the experiment is an artificial situation. The main criticism of experiments is that they set up artificial situations and produce results that are true of the experiment, but may not be true of the real world outside the laboratory. Researchers who prefer to study animals in their natural habitat often criticize research on animals in laboratories or zoos. People who prefer to study human beings in natural settings often make the same criticisms of laboratory research on humans. In both cases the criticism is that using an experimental method distorts the behaviour that is being studied.

Control versus naturalism
The more you can control variables in research, the more you can be certain about what is causing what. But the more you control variables the more artificial will be the situation you create. The more naturalistic your research, the more you can be sure that the research isn't producing distorted and misleading results. However, since you are not in control of all the variables in naturalistic research it is harder to determine which variable is causing what effects.

Choosing between control and naturalism

Research into social, psychological and animal behaviour varies according to how far researchers want to achieve naturalism and how far they want to achieve control. For social and psychological research you can think of this in terms of the diagram shown in Figure 4.2.

```
High on control

                    Laboratory experiments
              Questionnaires with closed questions
              Questionnaires with open questions
                    Structured interviews
                   Unstructured interviews
                        Observation where people
                        know they are being observed
                            Observation where people do not
                            know they are being observed
Low on control
Low on naturalism                              High on naturalism
```

Figure 4.2 The location of various research methods on the 'naturalism'–'control' scale

 Control and naturalism in your project

How you do this activity will depend on what kind of research you propose. First identify where on the graph your methods are likely to be. Will you be giving priority to controlling variables, or priority to doing naturalistic research? Or will you be adopting some compromise position?

Whatever your methods, you should make notes that answer the following questions.

▶ You may not be able to give very full answers to these questions now, but you may have to when you write up your project.

1 How would you show that you had attempted to control variables?

2 How would you respond to criticism that all your research discovered was how people, animals or things behaved when they were being researched, rather than in their natural settings?

Quantitative and qualitative research

Quantitative research is the kind where you measure things or count them, perhaps use statistical tests on your data, and then write up the results using tables, figures, graphs and bar charts. **Qualitative** research usually results in verbal descriptions, and might use quotations from people you interviewed or pictures of things happening. All research contains some verbal description and most involves some counting, so the difference between qualitative and quantitative research is often a matter of degree.

Sometimes people make the mistake of thinking that all naturalistic research is always primarily qualitative, and experimental research is always primarily quantitative. While it is true that experiments are usually arranged so that the results are given in numbers, the results of some experiments may be purely descriptive. Similarly, some kinds of naturalistic research, particularly in the fields of ecology or natural history, produce mainly quantitative results. So we have four kinds of research:

	Experimental	Naturalistic
Quantitative	Most laboratory experiments	For example: observations of people in ordinary settings using an observation schedule so that different kinds of behaviour can be classified, recorded and counted
Qualitative	Rare: experiments where there is nothing to count	Participant observation research where the researcher learns what it is like to be an 'insider' and describes this for readers

▶ Think of 'experimental' and 'naturalistic', and 'quantitative' and 'qualitative' as opposite ends of two scales – not as watertight compartments.

A naturalistic and largely quantitative study

In order to provide a contrast with the laboratory experiment described earlier, we shall now look at a piece of naturalistic research, but one that is largely quantitative in method. The example will also be used to illustrate the common situation where the researcher doesn't know what there is to research until he or she has actually done some research. For this reason the example starts with 'stage 1' of the project.

Stage 1:

A psychosocial investigation into territorial behaviour on Southend Beach

Comment

This is a very open-ended title because the researcher doesn't know yet what she will find that will be interesting to study. 'Psychosocial' indicates that she is interested in the sociological and psychological factors influencing the way in which people select and use positions on the beach.

Method

Observation between 8 a.m. and 2 p.m. daily for five days, with photographs from two fixed points every half-hour. Notes on anything that seems relevant. Records of a.m. and p.m. temperatures and of wind direction and speed (available from the Town Hall).

Since this is a project about positioning, photographs are an ideal way of making records. The weather records are important because, apart from social and psychological factors, the weather seems to be one of the two most likely influences on positioning. The other is the state of the tide, but this will automatically be recorded in the photographs. In a psychosocial project the weather and the tide will be a source of confounding variables. These cannot be controlled, but they can be 'controlled for' by recording them.

▶ Five days between 8 a.m. and 2 p.m. is what this researcher can afford in terms of research time.

Resources

Camera with wide-angle lens; film; notebook; multiple copies of map of beach; records from Town Hall.

▶ Both for classifying and for measuring it is necessary to have clear criteria and to use them in the same way all the time.

Analysis

By classifying people and groups into different types (such as young, old, male, female, families, friendship groups). By transferring information from photographs to map. By measuring the distances between groups on the beach.

At this stage in the project the researcher is simply looking for patterns and she may try various lines of analysis until she finds one that seems to make sense. Whatever she does, she is likely to:

- classify: people into types, behaviour into types, parts of the beach into different types of area;
- measure: distances between individuals/groups, and between them and important features of the beach, time elapsed.

So far, the research has been only descriptive, but what might the next stage of the project be? It would not be long before the researcher came up with some hypotheses that could be tested. One hypothesis, for example, might be that:

> the smaller the population on the beach, the greater the distance between individuals/groups.

With the data collected, the hunch could be tested from the photographs and the maps. However, if you know anything about bathing beaches you will know that things are seldom as simple as this.

Notice that so much of what the researcher has focused on so far can be measured and the results expressed in numbers: it is quantitative research.

In addition, the researcher might perhaps like to focus on the strategies people use to claim sections of beach for themselves, using windbreaks, loud music, rowdy ball-games, walls of sand and so on. She might then use her original notes as a starting point and then go on to make more observations of this kind. These observations are unlikely to result in quantitative data, but rather in verbal, qualitative descriptions – perhaps illustrated by some photographs. It may be that she decides to make these kinds of observations the main focus of her research, and to write a project that is therefore largely qualitative.

There is even a possibility here for some experimentation. For example, the researcher might gather together a group of friends to join the other people on the beach. By asking them to sit down in particular places, or to behave in particular ways, she could test some of her ideas out experimentally.

 Qualitative or quantitative

Tick the grid below to decide whether a largely quantitative or a largely qualitative method would be best for the projects listed. If you tick both columns then explain to yourself which bits of the research would be quantitative and which qualitative.

	Quantitative	Qualitative
Investigate office design in relation to productivity		
Investigate the impact of a new bypass on traffic in a village		
Investigate the role of dance among the teenage population of West Yorkshire		
Investigate customer satisfaction with a new chocolate bar		
Investigate customer satisfaction with the bar area of a new leisure centre		
Investigate the meaning of bullying among school children		
Investigate the reasons why people choose particular hotels to stay in		
Your own project title		

Review

By now you should have some idea of whether your research is going to be:

- descriptive/exploratory – to describe what happens and possibly to make suggestions for further research;
- explanatory and theory-testing – to draw some conclusions as to the validity of a suggested explanation;
- applied – to make some recommendations for future decisions.

You should also know whether you will design your research particularly to:

- control situations/create artificial situations to study; or
- use naturally occurring situations to study, disrupting them as little as possible

and whether you will use methods that produce:

- mainly quantitative data; or
- mainly qualitative data.

 Getting a fix on your methods

Look at the text in the review box. Have you made up your mind about these things? We suggest that you don't proceed any further with this chapter until you have. You might like to look back at the preceding pages to help you make up your mind, or seek advice from a tutor.

In the next chapter we shall be giving you more detail on particular research techniques. Before you proceed, however, it is worth looking at the main criteria against which research is judged (or evaluated).

▶ If the assessment specifications for your project ask you to write an evaluation of your own research, pay particular attention to this section.

▶ Some research is likely also to be judged in terms of the practical usefulness of the results, or the amount of new knowledge it adds to an academic discipline. However, these are rarely important criteria for student research. For student research the additional criterion is how much you learned from doing the project.

▶ It is much easier to define invalidity than validity.

CRITERIA FOR JUDGING RESEARCH

The most important standards, or criteria, against which research is judged are:

- validity,
- reliability,
- representativeness,
- objectivity,
- ethical standards (see Chapter 2).

Validity

The term **validity** is the closest most research methodologists come to saying 'true'. Like truth, validity is a difficult concept and it is probably best approached by asking what 'invalidity' might mean. We hope the diagram in the box will help you.

> #### Sources of invalidity: an example
> The student researcher has conducted some interviews with men and with women, has analysed the results, and has come to the conclusion that women are more frightened of crime than men. The researcher is a woman. There are many ways in which the conclusion could be invalid. Figure 4.3 shows some possibilities.
>
>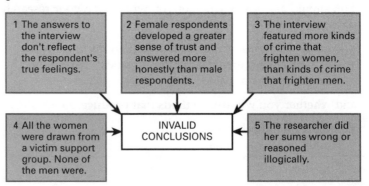

Figure 4.3 Possible reasons for invalid conclusions

Problems 1 and 2 relate to what is sometimes called **content validity**. For content validity the data must show what the researcher claims it shows. Here the data is said to show the respondents' fears of crime, but in 1 it simply doesn't and in 2 it may for women but not for men. Problems 1 and 2 are also variations of what is called **interviewer effect**: the respondent's answer depends on who the interviewer is and how he or she behaves. In 2 the gender of the interviewer is a **con-**

founding variable. Problems 2 and 3 are problems of **unreliability** because the interview gets different responses where it should get the same responses, or the same where it should get different ones (for more on reliability see below). Problem 4 is a problem of **representativeness** – this is dealt with in more detail below, but note how having experienced crime or not becomes a confounding variable here. Problem 5 hasn't got any special name but it obviously leads to an invalid conclusion.

Note that if the researcher chose to change her conclusion a little she might (or might not) make it valid. For example, problem 4 would not apply were her conclusion to be changed to: 'Women from victim support groups fear crime more than men who are not members of victim support groups'; likewise problem 2 would not apply to the conclusion: 'Respondents who have developed trust in the interviewer disclose their feelings more honestly' or problem 3 to the conclusion: 'On the questions asked in the interview, women reported more fear of crime than men'.

▶ The validity of a conclusion may depend on how the conclusion is phrased.

Since there are so many ways in which a piece of research can be invalid, you will never be able to claim that yours is valid. What you must do is to think of the possibilities for invalidity, try to avoid them, and, once the research is complete, investigate whether you have avoided them.

▶ Experimental researchers tend to claim that naturalistic research is invalid because it fails to control variables. Naturalistic researchers tend to claim that experimental research is invalid because it is artificial.

Reliability

The idea of **reliability** is most at home in the science laboratory, so let's start there. If you had a thermometer that gave various readings between 80°C and 100°C when placed in different bowls of boiling water, it would be an unreliable thermometer. Reliability means giving the same reading in the same circumstances. In much the same way, if you were using a questionnaire to test people's knowledge of geography, and you administered it to some people who read English well and others who read English badly, then the results might tell you more about the ability to read English than about knowledge of geography. In that respect it would be invalid – like problem 1 in Figure 4.3 – and it would also be an unreliable questionnaire, because it would work in different ways for different people who might have the same amount of knowledge of geography.

▶ Questionnaires, interview schedules, content analysis frames and so on are often called 'instruments', being comparable to the instruments used in a laboratory.

Using unreliable methods or instruments always leads to invalidity. However, highly reliable instruments do not guarantee validity. For example, if your thermometer always registered 80°C when placed in boiling water, it would be reliable but wrong, and would result in an invalid reading. In much the same way, those people who disapprove of intelligence tests will agree that they are reliable – because the same person will get much the same score on a second test – but claim that they are invalid, because they don't test 'intelligence'.

> ### Reliability
>
> It may help you to think about reliability as:
>
> > getting the same result when repeated in the same circumstances.

Sometimes reliability can be checked by using two methods to obtain the same information: two thermometers to measure the same heated water; two questions asking for the same information on a questionnaire; a second interview on the same topic. Sometimes reliability is checked by seeing if several judges agree. For example, if you wanted to judge whether the aggression shown by people on a video tape was high, medium or low, you might ask a panel of judges to decide, rather as judges decide marks in ice-skating competitions.

Unfortunately when instruments or judges disagree, it is rarely an easy matter to decide which is right.

▶ In the example of judging degrees of aggression, the important point is not what is the right judgement, but whether judgements are being made consistently.

Representativeness and generalizations

Any research you do will result first and foremost in conclusions about the people, animals or objects you actually studied, at the time, in the place and in the way that you studied them. However, the purpose of most research is to make generalizations that will stand for other people (animals, objects) at other times and in other places. **Representativeness** is the key to making generalizations. In the box on invalidity, the example was given of research on fear of crime conducted among female members of a victim support group. Having all been victims of crime, these women are most unlikely to be representative of women who have not been victims of crime, but they may be representative of other women victims.

You probably have a good common-sense notion of what representativeness means. In Chapter 6 we shall discuss the technicalities of choosing representative samples to study.

▶ You can think of **representativeness** in terms of one group 'standing for' a larger group. In so far as the group you study stands for other groups, you can generalize from the one to the other.

▶ Samples are never *simply* representative. They are always representative *of something*. Women from a victim support group may not be representative of all women with regard to the fear of crime but they may be representative of all women in victim support groups.

Objectivity

The last of the important criteria for judging research is **objectivity**.

The term **objectivity** actually covers two separate concepts. First there is **objective** as opposed to **biased** or **prejudiced**. It is obviously important not to let your prejudices cloud your research. Second there is **objective** – meaning **public** and **open**, as opposed to **subjective**, meaning **private** and **hidden**. Both meanings of objectivity are important for researchers.

Good research is said to produce 'objective' knowledge. This means that researchers give a full account of their methods, their data and their reasoning. This doesn't mean that they necessarily come to the right conclusions. It does mean that the conclusions they come to can be properly checked by others. In the long run it is more likely that better knowledge will be produced where the conclusions can be checked by others, because this means that faulty conclusions can be identified and disregarded.

> ### Review: The main standards against which research is evaluated
> Your research will be evaluated primarily for:
>
> * validity – or at least the absence of obvious invalidity;
> * reliability of the methods used;
> * representativeness as the basis for making generalizations;
> * objectivity – in the sense that readers can check the conclusions for themselves;
> * ethical standards (see Chapter 2).
>
> We are not going to ask you to check your own research against these criteria yet. But later we shall do so.

CHAPTER SUMMARY

This chapter looked broadly at different kinds of research and the different kinds of methods that are associated with them. These were:

* exploratory/descriptive research contrasted with explanatory and theory-testing research;
* pure research contrasted with applied research;
* experimental research (with the emphasis on controlling variables) contrasted with naturalistic research;
* quantitative research contrasted with qualitative research.

We also looked at the major criteria against which research is judged. We shall ask you to look at these again later.

5 More on methods

► In this chapter we shall look in more detail at some of the research methods that you are most likely to use. These include:

- questionnaires;
- content analysis;
- interviews;
- non-participant observation;
- participant observation.

Experimental methods in laboratory science were dealt with in Chapter 4.

Chapter objectives
After working through this chapter you will be able to:

▌ identify a range of different research methods;

▌ determine which ones are appropriate for your project;

▌ decide which methods to use;

▌ find out more about the methods you have chosen.

CLASSIFICATION AND DEFINITION

Whatever methods you choose, you will have to devise and use precise categories and tell your readers exactly how you define them. Some categories come virtually ready-made. For example, 'male' and 'female', '16-year-old', and 'traffic warden' all have well-known and easily recognizable meanings. Others need more precise definitions, such as 'working class' or 'young person', or 'violent episode'.

 Categories and definitions in your project

First make a list of all the important categories you are going to use in your research. Then, for each of them, provide precise definitions that would enable someone else to use the term in the same way as you are using it.
    For example: Hedgerows

Type A – a hedgerow containing more than five species of shrub/tree and occasional standard trees
Type B – as above, without standard trees

    For example: Traffic

'Heavy traffic' – more than fifteen vehicles per minute
'Medium traffic' – between five and fourteen vehicles per minute
'Light traffic' – fewer than five vehicles per minute

Test whether your definitions work properly by asking other people to apply them, and checking whether they use them in the same way.

QUESTIONNAIRES AND OTHER PROFORMAS

You know what a questionnaire is: a list of questions. In this sense a questionnaire is similar to a job application form, a form for making tax returns, a multiple choice examination or even a shopping list that you tick when you have bought the items listed. If you think of questionnaires as proformas for eliciting and recording information, you can see what they have in common with other proformas.

▶ Standard blank forms are sometimes called **proformas**. **Questionnaires** are proformas for eliciting and recording information.

	Shopping list	Job application form	Research questionnaire filled in by interviewer	Research questionnaire filled in by respondent
Who asks the questions?				
Who has to understand the questions?				
Who has to answer the questions?				
Who has to understand the answers?				

Different kinds of proforma

Fill in the grid above with appropriate answers. Think of a shopping list as a set of instructions ('buy this') and questions ('have you bought this?').

Other commonly used proformas in research include tables for recording the results of experiments, maps for recording the location of, say, species in a field, observation schedules for recording the occurrence of particular kinds of behaviour by animals or people and content frames for analysing media products.

In each case, the proforma will only be workable if:

- whoever needs to know what the question/instruction means does know what the question/instruction means;
- whoever needs to know what the answer means does know what the answer means.

Designing proformas is an exercise in good communication. We shall restrict our remarks to the three types of proforma most commonly used in research: questionnaires, observation schedules and content analysis frames.

▶ Using questionnaires or interviews assumes that the respondents can and will give you the information you want. People are often unreliable witnesses to their own behaviour, or know less than you expect. They may invent answers just to avoid looking silly.

▶ Techniques used for choosing samples of people to whom a questionnaire should be given are discussed in Chapter 6.

Questionnaires

Who completes it?

Questionnaires are very commonly used in research with people. They vary according to whether they are to be:

- filled in by the respondent unaided;
- filled in by the respondent in the presence of an interviewer who can give clarification;
- filled in by an interviewer who will interpret the respondent's words to match the answers provided.

 Questionnaires in your research

Consider these options in terms of their advantages and disadvantages to the researcher and decide which technique you are going to use.

Kinds of question

Questions on questionnaires vary according to whether they are:

- closed – that is, with a limited set of options for answers provided (Yes/No/Don't know or Very much/Much/Not very much/Not at all); or
- open – allowing respondents to answer as they like and in their own words.

▶ An example of an open question:
'Please complete the following sentence: "When I think of old people I think. . . "'

Open and closed questions

Closed questions

Advantages: Closed questions result in sets of responses that are easy to count and manipulate statistically.

Disadvantages: Using closed questions assumes that you, the researcher, know in advance all the important answers respondents might give if they had the free choice you are not giving them. It imposes restrictions on how people can answer.

Open questions

Advantages: Open questions allow respondents to give the answers they want to give without imposing a restricted set of responses on them.

Disadvantages: Using open questions results in data that is usually very difficult to classify, count and manipulate statistically.

Questionnaires with open questions are often used in the preliminary and exploratory phase of research. Responses to these open questions may form the basis of a closed-question questionnaire that is used in a later stage of the research.

The choice between open and closed questions does not have to be made for a questionnaire as a whole. It is better to make the choice for particular questions. Some questions are by their nature 'closed', such as: 'Are you male or female?'; 'Are you single, married, divorced/separated, widowed?'

▶ In multiple choice questions, an even number of alternatives is preferred to an odd one. This prevents people simply opting for the middle choice.

Scaling responses on a questionnaire

One useful way of framing a closed question is to provide answers that can be scaled. For example:

For each of the following statements would you:

Strongly agree Agree Disagree Strongly disagree

Answers that have been scaled in this way can be subjected to a wide variety of statistical tests.

Representative check questions

Your research may not be directly concerned with whether your respondent is male or female, younger or older and so on. It is wise, however, to include some such questions on a questionnaire in order to be able to check how far your respondents have been representative.

▶ See Chapter 6, 'Representativeness in retrospect', p. 95.

Understandable questions

It goes without saying that the questions on a questionnaire must be understandable to those who have to answer them. This is even more important where there is no interviewer to explain or clarify them. However, it is often quite difficult to write questions that are understandable.

Piloting questions

As a student researcher you probably cannot afford the luxury of trying out the first version of your questionnaire on real respondents. What you should do, however, is to get some obstructive colleagues to help you by doing their best to misunderstand your questions. Rewrite the questions in the light of their reactions.

Avoiding leading questions

All questions are leading, in the sense that they lead to an answer. Closed questions are, of course, more leading than open questions because they lead to one of a restricted range of answers. However the term 'leading questions' refers to questions phrased in such a way that it seems to the respondent that there is an answer that will please or impress the researcher. Consider the following question:

Are you one of those people who is ambitious and go-ahead rather than someone who is prepared to let other people walk all over them?

It is pretty obvious that in saying 'yes' the respondent will give a much better impression of themselves than in saying 'no'. But we could reverse the effect:

> Are you one of those people who pursue their ambitions irrespective of the harm they do to others rather than someone who takes others' needs into consideration?

These are gross examples of leading questions. In order to avoid leading questions entirely you need to know a great deal about the kinds of people who will complete the questionnaire and what impression they might want to convey in their answers.

► Leading questions may affect the validity of your research. You find out what images people wish to convey about themselves, which is probably not what you set out to find.

Design and layout

As with any other kind of form, if the questionnaire is to be filled in by the respondent its overall design is crucially important. It should be clearly titled with some explanation of what the questionnaire is for and how the results will be used. It must contain clear instructions, be easy to read and, as far as possible, pleasant to read. If you have access to desk-top publishing facilities, use them for producing questionnaires. Ensure a simple but attractive design and layout.

► Designing questionnaires is a very skilled and difficult task. There are many excellent reference books on questionnaire design.

Code of conduct

 The contract with the respondent

If you are going to use a questionnaire, take some time to compose the explanation and the promises that will appear at the head of the questionnaire. You might attempt this task by amending and completing the material in the box below so that it suits your particular situation:

► Refer to the notes on ethical codes of conduct you made in Chapter 2.

> This questionnaire is part of a research project to .... Your cooperation in completing the questionnaire will be of great value to me. Please do not put your name or any other identifying information on the questionnaire. Although I will know who has completed each questionnaire, this information will not be disclosed to anyone else by me, and there is no other way in which anyone could find out your identity.

► Refer to the notes on ethical codes of conduct you made in Chapter 2.

The length of a questionnaire

Most people in any situation will not be prepared to spend long periods of time filling in your questionnaire, so you should keep it as short as possible. This will mean making some hard choices. In making these choices, it may help to consider another limit on the length of questionnaires. As a general rule,

> the smaller the number of people who complete questionnaires the fewer the number of different answers you should allow for.

For example, let's suppose that 'occupation' is an important variable in your research. In your questionnaire you allow the respondent to tick one of 30 kinds of occupation. If you only have 50 respondents then providing 30 occupations is a waste of your time and theirs. With 50 respondents, you won't know whether the fact that at least 20 of the occupations were ticked by no one at all is a matter of significance or a matter of chance. The only way in which you can use the answer to this question will be to reclassify the occupations into two or three broader types. You would have done better to provide these broader types in the questionnaire in the first place, making it much shorter and simpler.

Postal questionnaires

If someone sent you a questionnaire through the post, would you complete it and send it back? For the vast majority of respondents the answer would be 'no'. Sending questionnaires by post, even with stamped and addressed return envelopes and even with telephone follow-ups, usually results in low rates of return, often below 10 per cent. What's worse is that the people who do complete and return the questionnaires are usually unrepresentative of the sample from whom you wanted to collect information. The only time you should use postal questionnaires is where you have already gained a firm commitment from the respondents to complete them. This will usually be where you are collecting information from a fairly small number of people and you don't have time to interview them.

If you are using questionnaires and you will be with the respondents when they are filled in, then you also need to read the section on interviews later in this chapter.

Observation schedules

Coding instructions for observation of nurse behaviour

T = Talks	S = Silent
TA = Answers question	SS = Unmoving
TQ = Asks question	SG = Gestures
TI = Gives instruction	SM = Walking
TO = Other verbalization	

Observations every minute on the minute. Write the appropriate code on the time grid.

In the box above are some instructions for a researcher observing nurse behaviour; there would be another set of instructions for observing patients. In effect this is just another closed-question questionnaire, but it is one filled in by the researcher. It asks: 'What is the nurse doing at this time?'; 'Is the nurse answering a question or asking a question?' and so on.

► In this piece of research, part of the problem of representativeness has been solved by observing every minute on the minute – systematic sampling. But how were representative nurses, wards and hospitals selected?

You may have guessed that there are problems in using this schedule. These are problems of classifying behaviour and of using the same definitions consistently. For example, in reality it is not always at all clear what 'asking a question' means. Sometimes it may mean the nurse saying, 'How are you today?' or more significantly, 'Where is the pain?' Sometimes a nurse's silence means: 'I am angry' or 'I am upset'.

This kind of problem occurs in questionnaire research as well. While two respondents may answer 'yes' to the same question, they may have interpreted the question differently, and mean different things by their yesses. When we are doing questionnaire research this problem is usually hidden from view, but when the researcher is both the questioner and the respondent it becomes very obvious.

For this particular observation schedule to be workable, there would have to be much more information provided about how to classify bits of nurse behaviour, probably illustrated with examples from real wards, or even better, with video clips. If more than one observer was to be involved, then it would be important that all observers used the same definitions and classified the same piece of behaviour in the same way. To accomplish this, quite extensive training might be necessary.

▶ If the same observer classified the same behaviour differently on different occasions the observer would be **unreliable**. If two different observers were consistent in their classifications but different from each other, they would both be reliable, but the overall results would be invalid.

Observation schedules, then, are very much like questionnaires. The questions or instructions must be clearly understood by those who have to answer them, and understood in the same way by different people using them.

Content analysis frameworks

Content analysis is a technique of research usually used where the subject matter is text, or sound or televised materials. A content analysis framework is a kind of observation schedule for dealing with printed or broadcast materials or, if you prefer, a kind of questionnaire asking the researcher questions about this material.

▶ This wouldn't be a particularly good piece of research as it stands, because without knowing how the occupations of white people are portrayed in the same papers, we couldn't say anything significant about how black people were portrayed. So the research should cover how occupations are portrayed for people in general so that the two groups can be compared. In other words, we need an 'experimental group' and a 'control group'.

Suppose, for example, a student researcher was interested in the way in which black people were portrayed in newspapers. A simple content framework might deal with the way in which black people were portrayed in terms of occupation. However, since newspapers are complicated publications, with front pages, sports pages, supplements and adverts, our researcher would probably also be interested in where in the newspaper black people were portrayed. He or she might then develop a coding system something like this:

Occupation indicated	Location
For example:	For example:
No occupation indicated	Front page
Unemployed	Back page
Criminal/Prisoner	Other home news
Third-World peasant	Overseas news
Blue-collar	Sports
White-collar	Media

Thought of as a questionnaire, this content analysis frame asks: 'Is someone mentioned? If so, is that person's occupation indicated? And from what ethnic group does the person come? And where in the newspaper did the mention occur?'

Paper: *The Times*, 3 January
Location: Front page

Table 5.1 Content analysis frame showing how black people are portrayed in newspapers.

White	Occupation	Black	Occupation
7	Politicians	1	Mental patient
2	Criminals	1	Criminal
1	Sportsperson	2	Sportspersons
3	Entertainers	1	Unemployed
3	Unemployed		
3	Managers		
19		5	

Note: Story about youth unemployment: picture with four youths – three white and one black.

In this particular content analysis the only things that can be counted are mentionings in particular parts of the newspaper. Other kinds of content analysis can go further in quantification by measuring the column inches of print devoted to a particular topic or the seconds in shot of a particular kind of person on the television.

► Research based on content analysis also raises questions about what constitutes a representative sample of newspapers.

As with observation schedules, there will be tricky problems to solve regarding definition and classification.

Content analysis can also be used as a technique for analysing the transcripts of tape-recorded interviews. Something like this is described in Chapter 10.

► See Chapter 10, p. 148.

INTERVIEWS

Levels of structure

Interviews are a very common research instrument used by student researchers. The main way in which interviews vary is according to how far they are pre-structured and how far they are allowed to unfold and develop differently with each interviewee.

► Interviews are not simply alternatives to questionnaires; many interviews involve a questionnaire.

Structured

The interviewer reads the questions from a questionnaire in the same way and in the same order for each respondent and records the answers.

Unstructured

The interviewer allows the interview to develop according to the interests of the interviewee and/or along interesting lines that crop up during the interview.

► In essence, **structured** means asking each person the same question in the same way. **Unstructured** means treating each person as a unique individual.

There are many intermediate points between these two extremes.

For example, there may be standard questions but asked in a different order for different respondents; there may be a mix of standard questions plus some time allowed for the interviewer to ask questions that he or she devises on the spot; there may be a checklist of topics with the interviewer deciding on the spot what questions to ask in what order and so on.

► The advantages and disadvantages are another version of the choice the researcher must make between control and naturalism that was discussed in Chapter 4.

Structured interviews

Advantages: Each respondent is asked the same questions in the same way. Therefore a direct point-by-point comparison can be made between respondents. This will be especially important if the responses are to be counted and treated in numerical terms.

Disadvantages: A structured interview assumes that the researcher knows in advance what the important questions are. The standardized approach chosen may turn out to be more appropriate for some respondents than others. There are no opportunities to follow up interesting issues with particular respondents.

Unstructured interviews

Advantages: Respondents are allowed to express themselves in their own unique way, therefore more authentic responses are likely. The interviewer can adjust the language, the pace and the sequencing of the interview to make it suitable for different respondents. Unstructured interviewing does not need the researcher to know in advance what the important questions are.

Disadvantages: Since each interview will be unique, making point-by-point comparisons between them may be difficult. It will be difficult to convert responses into numbers for quantitative treatment.

 When to use structured and when to use an unstructured approach

Look at the following kinds of research and decide when a more structured and when a less structured approach would be appropriate.

	More structured	Less structured
Research to discover how often people go to the doctor	☐	☐
Research to discover what influences people in deciding to see the doctor	☐	☐
Research comparing how three different firms market their product	☐	☐
Research to discover what managers think makes a 'good employee'	☐	☐

More structured   Less structured

Research in the same project as
above to discover how many
employees share the same
views as the managers from
the first set of interviews   ☐   ☐

It is difficult to give precise advice about when to use more or less structured interviewing, but here are some rules of thumb:

- When your research involves asking 'how many?', a structured approach is likely to be more appropriate.
- When your research aim is to understand the meanings people give to their experience, a less structured approach is likely to be more appropriate.
- When your research is exploratory, or in an initial exploratory phase before you are sure what's worth researching, a less structured approach is more likely to be appropriate.
- When clarity is important, for instance in interviewing a manager about his or her organization, a structured interview is appropriate, perhaps with time for unstructured discussion at the end.

Unstructured followed by structured interviewing
Sonia was studying what young people knew and thought about illegal drugs. She did three long unstructured interviews. This taught her about the kinds of language these young people used about drugs and sensitized her to the drug issues that were important to them. On this basis she drew up a questionnaire that she used for much shorter structured interviews with another twenty young people.

Arranging the interview

It is very unlikely that being interviewed by you will be one of the main priorities in someone else's life. In selecting your interviewees you should ensure that the individuals actually want to take part. The selection of an individual who genuinely does not want to be part of your research is very likely to lead to disappointment and frustration.

Interviewees are entitled to have some idea of what is going to be required of them. It is not necessary to discuss all the details of the research, but you should cover the topic area, the aims of the research and what is likely to be done with the outcomes, as well as the mechanics of the interview such as its length, how it will be recorded and where it will occur. You must then stick to these.

► See Chapter 2, pp. 4–21 on research ethics.

Credentials and identification

You should not to go into a public place and simply ask people

► Look after yourself. There are potential dangers involved in approaching people you do not know, particularly if you intend to visit them at their home to conduct the interview. You must take suitable precautions, including informing people of your activities and whereabouts, and possibly visiting in pairs rather than alone.

► Refer to the notes on ethical codes of conduct that you made in Chapter 2, pp. 19–20.

questions. You may find that you will need to seek permission from someone in authority, for example, your local council or shopping centre manager. When interviewing strangers you should have verifiable identification. Your school or college may provide you with this or, alternatively, it may be provided by whoever you have to ask permission from.

Code of practice for interviews

As part of gaining permission it is important that interviewees are fully aware of the reasons behind the research and the part they are going to play in it. Many researchers produce a code of practice that they discuss and agree with their interviewees. This tends to be done when there are manageable numbers of interviewees rather than a very large sample.

The code of practice basically explains the rights of the interviewee, and could be considered as an informal contract that will allow the process to be undertaken and the outcomes to be utilized.

 Your code of practice for interviews

If you are using interviews as a research strategy, fill in the blanks in this code of practice. Amend the code if it does not quite fit your situation.

► A code of practice is also a contract. It is your promise to those involved in your research. You should always keep these promises.

Code of practice

1 The aim of this interview is to obtain information and ideas on . . .

2 The findings will be included in a report for . . .

3 The identity of individuals will not be disclosed. However, the interviewee's age, sex and . . . may be used.

4 Interviews will take place only at these times and places: . . .

5 All interviews will be prearranged.

6 There will be no fee for interviewees.

7 Interviewees will have the right to terminate the interview at any time and/or choose not to answer some or all of the questions.

8 The interpretation of the interview will be discussed with . . . prior to presentation in the final written report.

9 During an interview the interviewee may ask for statements to be regarded as 'off the record'. These must never be quoted in the final report.

You will need to think about with whom you are agreeing the code of practice: interviewees, their employers (if they are in a workplace), their parents (if they are children)? How will this influence the points to be agreed, and how many extra matters will you need to agree to ensure good practice?

Another point to remember regarding the code of practice is that you will need to develop a method of identifying any data that interviewees ask to be kept confidential or non-attributable, and for recording any other requests that interviewees may make about the use of data supplied by them.

The mechanics of interview

Making appointments

If appointments are to be made, these will have to be at mutually convenient times and at a place that is accessible both to interviewer and to interviewee. It is a fact that, however well organized you believe you are, confusion can occur over appointments, especially if the details are not put in writing or if they are organized through a third party. Our advice would be always to make appointments in writing and to ask for written confirmation. Make sure of the obvious details, that is: a time, a date, a place and sufficient information to indicate what the appointment is about.

Each interview will produce a lot of data and you must decide at what point you are going to use that data. This may determine how frequently appointments should occur. This is most important when you intend to carry out more than one interview with an individual in order to check whether his or her opinion has changed over a period of time.

The location of the interview

Sometimes you will carry out an interview in a place specified by an interviewee, such as his or her office. If you can choose the location, then you should try to ensure the following:

- The location of the interview must be accessible to both parties. This is not always easy and you may have to seek someone's permission to use such a place.
- It is important that you are not disturbed by other people, or by the telephone – this is a particular problem when interviews take place in offices, and you may not be able to ensure it. Interviews that are frequently interrupted are frustrating and often difficult to analyse.
- The location of the interview must be conducive to good communication. For an interview that may last up to an hour you will need to consider comfortable seating, pleasant temperature and lighting, and perhaps the availability of refreshments.

▶ If you are going to interview in the street, your interviews must be short – preferably no longer than ten minutes.

Any factors that may influence the outcome of the interview and the physical and mental comfort of the interviewee should be addressed. It is your responsibility to check that you have the best possible environment for your interview and that you do this well before the interview has started.

Telephone interviewing

Commercial research firms are increasingly using the telephone to conduct interviews: often one call to agree the interview and a convenient time, and another to conduct the interview. However, sometimes it may be necessary to send a letter in between the two calls in order to show your credentials, and present the interviewee with a code of conduct and an explanation of the research. Apart from the cost of the calls, telephone interviewing is a very convenient method, especially for closed-question interviews.

► Telephone interviewing only gives you access to people who have telephones. If this makes your sample unrepresentative, you could in addition arrange face-to-face interviews with people without telephones.

Recording the interview

Some interviews will be conducted using a questionnaire. Recording these will mainly mean you ticking the right boxes, or filling in the right blanks, always checking to see if you are correctly recording what the respondent says.

Less structured interviews are more difficult to record. Do not underestimate how many words will be spoken in a relatively brief interview of thirty minutes. It is essential that those words are recorded accurately because they are your research data and if you choose to miss out a few sentences then you may change your data in a manner that is entirely unacceptable.

► The more unstructured an interview, the more difficult it is to record.

Remember that it is entirely reasonable that another researcher, or indeed the person who is going to assess your work, would ask to see your original data in order to check whether he or she agrees with your interpretation.

Verbatim notes taken by yourself

The cheapest way to record your data is for you to write down what is being said. For unstructured interviews this is extremely difficult. It slows down the discussion; it breaks trains of thought and it encourages the use of abbreviations and handwriting that is almost impossible to decipher later. The temptation is to omit parts of the conversation, but this will lead to inaccuracies.

If this is going to be your method of recording then allow yourself plenty of time in the interview and check with the interviewee that you are reflecting his or her comments accurately. In general, the more precise your questions and the more structured your interview, the easier it will be to make good verbatim notes.

Using a scribe

Because of the difficulties of both conducting and recording an interview simultaneously, you might find it helpful to introduce a third person to record the conversation – providing this is acceptable to the interviewee. Agreement to use a scribe must be gained before the interview.

Tape recording

Tape recording the interview is probably the simplest and most accurate way of gathering data. However you need to be aware of some of the pitfalls. These include the following:

- Many people are worried about being recorded, particularly if they were not aware that this was going to occur.
- Tape recorders do not always function properly. Cheap battery tape recorders produce substantial background noise, which may make it difficult to interpret the recording.
- Many perfectly intelligent people find the process of working a tape recorder extremely difficult. You must make sure that you can work the tape recorder before the interview starts. Make sure that there is a tape in the machine, that it is switched on, and that you have a spare tape.
- In addition to background noise on the tape, it is likely that the recorder will pick up noise in the room or immediately outside it, such as telephones, traffic or other conversations. It is important that you minimize these as far as possible.
- It is important to position the microphone so as to ensure that it picks up the speech of both the interviewer and the interviewee. You must test this for every interview that you undertake.
- Remember to keep accurate records of each interview. You may choose to keep a written log whereby you identify each tape with a reference and write a brief description of each section of the interview while at the same time keeping a note of the tape recorder counter numbers at the start and finish of each section. This is especially helpful if later you have to check the actual tape recording against a written transcription.

Making tape recordings anonymously

You may wish to allocate reference numbers or letters to your interviewees so that their identity is protected in your log. This is especially important if you have agreed confidentiality in your code of practice. The record of the identity of your interviewees and their allocated reference should be kept separate from the material that will be submitted to an assessor.

Remember that making a recording of the interview is only the first step in the data-collection process. Almost invariably you will have to transcribe some of your taped interview into a written document. This is very time consuming and initially quite difficult to do because of the speed of the spoken word. In addition, most people do not speak in sentences or paragraphs, and even with a good tape recording it can be difficult to know when to include features such as question marks or full stops, let alone paragraph breaks.

▶ Even rough and ready transcription takes about one hour's transcribing for each 15 minutes' interviewing.

Your behaviour during the interview

Apart from always being friendly and polite there are two quite contrary pieces of advice given to interviewers.

Avoiding an interviewer effect
Interviewers are advised that they should

> behave as far as possible in the same way towards each interviewee

and at the same time that they should

> try to establish a good relationship with each interviewee so that they can respond to each as a unique individual.

The balance between these two pieces of advice may be determined by the kind of interview you are conducting. For short, closed-question interviews in the street, the first advice would be sensible. For long, unstructured interviews on sensitive topics the second advice would be better.

The fact that contrary advice is given relates to a dilemma that faces any researcher who uses interview techniques. The dilemma is this: the interviewer wants to collect information that isn't influenced or distorted by the interviewer's presence or behaviour, and yet, for an interview, there has to be an interviewer. The first kind of advice tries to solve the problem by making sure that if there is an interviewer effect, it will be the same for each respondent – because the interviewer behaved in the same way towards each. The second piece of advice assumes that there will be an interviewer effect, but tries to overcome it by gaining the trust of the interviewee.

There is no satisfactory solution to this problem, but if you listen to tapes of your interviews you can often hear how you encourage or inhibit interviewees. You should comment on this in your research report.

OBSERVATION

Non-participant and participant observation

It is usual to think of observation on a scale running from fully non-participant to fully participant observation.

Fully non-participant
For example: observation from behind a one-way mirror; from a vantage point 'outside the action'; by a fly-on-the-wall video camera

Fully participant
The observer is a member of the group being studied and joins in with the action.

For non-participant observation there are important practical considerations about where you or the video camera needs to be in order to observe what is going on without disrupting what is happening. These are challenges that wildlife observers face all the time.

For the participant observer there is the problem of how to become a member of the group being studied, and at the same time not to disrupt what is being studied. There are many situations in which it is impossible, or undesirable, to attempt participant observation research. For example, a 25-year-old observer simply cannot become a **member** of a group of teenagers who hang around the Wimpy Bar. He or she might take a different kind of role in the same setting however: as another customer, or as a member of staff.

It is unwise for student researchers to become involved in any dangerous or illegal activities for the purpose of doing research.

▶ However tempting it may be, *don't* involve yourself in the dangerous or illegal activities of others for research purposes.

Ethical issues in observation research

Where the subjects of research are people, then the researcher often faces a difficult ethical dilemma. On the one hand, people have a right to be told that they are being observed. On the other hand, telling them may cause them to change their behaviour. There are many kinds of observation research that could not be done if the people being observed were told they were being observed. If you are going to do observation research you will have to think carefully about the ethics of informed consent. The grid below may help you.

 Ethical issues in observation research

Here are some examples of observation research. For each, decide where you would place them on the grid, and whether disclosure of your research intentions would spoil the research.

	Public places	**Private places**
Some risk of harm to those observed		
No risk of harm to those observed		

1 Observation of passenger behaviour on the platform of a railway station
2 Observation of customer–staff interchanges in a tourist information centre
3 Observation of talk and behaviour of a bank's employees in their lunch break
4 Observation of pupil–instructor interaction in a sports centre

5 Observation of litter-dropping behaviour of people in town centre

On the whole, the more public the location and the less harm done to those observed, the less it is ethically necessary to inform people that they are being observed. Possible harm should be limited by preserving anonymity for those observed, whether or not they are told that they are being studied.

In participant observation research, ethical dilemmas are generally more difficult to resolve. If you have gained membership of a group in the sort of way that people usually gain membership of groups, then it is a betrayal of trust to exploit that membership for research purposes. On the other hand, you may not be able to do any research at all if you explain what you are doing, and certainly won't be able to observe 'what normally happens' if you keep reminding people that you are researching them.

► In public places it is often impractical to inform people that they are being observed.

The ethics of participant observation

 Rights to know in participant observation research

Read the case study.

For her course, Lorna undertook a work-experience placement in a residential home for elderly people. The senior staff of the home knew that Lorna had to write an 'agency study' while she was there and agreed to this on condition that they saw the written-up report before it went for assessment. No one told the management that Lorna would be presenting her findings to other students as she went along. When Lorna first met the other staff in the home she was open about her research, although at that stage she didn't quite know what she would focus on. Thereafter, she became a 'colleague', and rarely reminded anyone that she was researching. No one told the elderly residents of the home that Lorna was doing research.

► Observation research often requires you to gain permission to observe from a third party who controls the space in which you are observing. You may need to be issued with identification and credentials.

First, consider who had a right to know about Lorna's research aims and activities and what they should know. Then consider what effect it would have if Lorna told everyone who had a right to know, and kept reminding them about it. How would you have resolved these dilemmas?

 Your code of conduct for observation research

► Even if you are not going to tell anyone you are researching about your intentions, you should still write a code of conduct for yourself.

If you are using observation research you should draft your code of conduct. Look at the codes of conduct for questionnaires and for interviews given earlier (pp. 62 and 68) and the notes on an ethical code of conduct you made in Chapter 2 (pp. 19–20). Then decide who you are going to write a code of conduct for – you may need different codes of conduct for different groups of people. Then write the code or codes of conduct.

Observation and recording

Observation schedules

Like interviews, observation may be structured or unstructured. We have already given you an example of an observation schedule for structured observation. Think of observation schedules as questionnaires for yourself, asking: 'What's happening now: is it (a), (b), (c) or (d)?' You might fill in the schedule directly as the action happens, or more indirectly by watching a video recording of the action.

Field notes

Unstructured observation means being around and keeping your eyes and ears open for anything relevant and interesting. If you are a participant observer, you can't keep breaking off from your role in the situation in order to write things down. You will therefore need to rely on your memory to a considerable degree and make what are called 'field notes' as quickly after the event as possible. Many participant observers find that they need to make frequent 'trips to the toilet' to write things down quickly before they forget them! Field notes made at the research location are usually brief and poorly written. It is essential that at the end of a period of observation you allocate some time to write them up neatly so that they will make sense in future.

Examples of observation research

To demonstrate the use of different types of observation techniques, let us take a particular example. Supposing we were responsible for deciding exactly where a seat should be placed at a beauty spot famous for its views.

First of all we need to establish that enough people visit the site to make it worthwhile to invest in the cost of the seat and its upkeep. So the first task would be to use an automatic counter to record the numbers of visitors to the beauty spot. Clearly this is non-participant observation.

Having established that enough people visit the site to make the placing of a seat worthwhile, the next step would be to make a record of where the majority of visitors actually stop to look at a particular view. You could take this step a little further and record separately those people who sit on the grass and those who lean against a tree at that point.

You may like to consider how many times you would have to repeat this by making your observations at different times of the day, in different seasons and in different weather conditions. You might also consider some of the other variables that could affect your decision about where to site the seat.

These observations can be undertaken from a distance and may be recorded on video tape with an operator in attendance. (A fixed video camera operated by remote control could miss some of the

▶ The most appropriate recording device for this purpose would be a map.

Figure 5.1 Map showing viewing point where seat is to be sited

activity that could be relevant to the decision about where to site the seat.)

A common method of indicating the number of times an identified activity occurs is by the use of a frequency recording grid. In this case, the area being observed is divided into sub-areas that are indicated on a recording sheet, normally in the shape of squares. As each activity occurs, a mark is made in the appropriate square. Figure 5.2 provides an example of the numbers of people who stopped in different places to look at a view.

Remember that the observer can influence the outcome of the activity. It seems likely that visitors would be influenced in some way if they saw a person with a clipboard watching them and then writing something down.

From Figure 5.2 we can see that most people stopped in squares 10, 11, 26 and 27 to look at the view, but can we be sure these squares mark the best view point or just the first place the visitors felt comfortable enough to stop after having seen the observer?

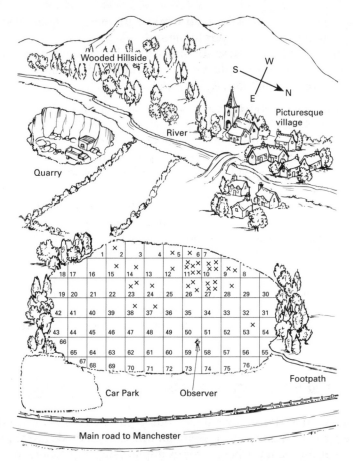

Figure 5.2 Map with frequency recording grid showing numbers of visitors to viewing point who stopped for more than 5 seconds (Saturday, 11 June between 2 p.m. and 6 p.m.)

More accurate answers could be obtained if you actually asked the people why they had chosen that spot and what they were looking at. To do this you could use a straightforward structured interview technique filling in a questionnaire with their answers. Or you could use a participant observation technique, taking the role of another sightseer and asking them questions more casually.

For a more experimental approach, you might temporarily place some seats and observe the reaction of the visitors if, or when, they used them, using the same non-participant observation technique as before.

As well as asking the people using the seats for their opinion of the suitability of their siting, you could leave questionnaires or comment sheets (not forgetting also to leave a pen or pencil) and a box for the replies that could be analysed later. There would almost certainly be a low response to this and therefore considerable doubt about whether those who responded were representative of all those visiting the spot.

You would also need to record the weather conditions to give greater understanding of any variance in numbers. You might also need to indicate any other major factors that were known to you that might have some bearing on the number of visitors – a major sporting event, such as the FA Cup Final, might well keep the num-

► Of course, you could simply ask them where they thought you ought to site the seat.

bers down, as would major road works with the consequent traffic delays on the approach roads to the site.

At the end of this project to establish the best place to site a seat at a beauty spot, you would have a collection of data that was both quantitative and qualitative. You will have:

- data on the numbers of visitors to the site, which could be shown as bar charts to indicate at what times or particular days of the week different numbers of visitors used the site;
- a number of frequency observation grids indicating how many visitors stopped in particular areas to look at the view;
- a collection of comments made by the visitors when asked why they had stopped at that particular point;
- a collection of video tapes showing how visitors use the site;
- a list of visitors' suggestions as to the best place to site the seat.

With the amount of time and effort that has gone into producing all this data, you should be able to identify the best place to site the seat. All that remains now is to design a research project to identify the best sort of seat!

USING SEVERAL METHODS

In the example above, several methods of research were used in the same project. You will have seen that different methods are appropriate for different purposes. For example, using a questionnaire to ask people where they stood to look at the view would not be a very appropriate method, since people are notoriously forgetful about their own behaviour. Observation is a much better method of discovering what people actually do. On the other hand, observing people rarely tells you about people's reasons or opinions; for this information, asking them is a better approach.

Triangulation

In addition to varying your methods to suit different purposes, data collected by one method can also be used to check data collected by another. You can have more confidence in a conclusion based on two or more different methods of research than you can in a conclusion based on one method of research alone. This is sometimes called 'triangulation by method'.

 Your methods

By now you should have a pretty good idea of what method or methods of research you are going to use in your project. Now is the time to find out more about that methodology. Talk to your tutor or use the library to investigate the research method further, before you apply the method to your research.

▶ On using the library, see Chapter 8.

CHAPTER SUMMARY

This chapter has looked at a range of research methods. These have included:

- questionnaires;
- content analysis;
- interviews – structured and unstructured;
- structured observation, with observation schedules;
- unstructured participant observation.

You will have noticed that these methods do not fall into watertight compartments. It doesn't greatly matter how you label your methods. What is important is that you choose the methods that will produce the best data for your purposes. Often this will mean using more than one method of data collection in the same project.

6 Choosing a sample or a case

WHY YOU MIGHT NEED A SAMPLE

► This chapter covers the issues of who, what and how many you should study.

People starting out on projects often have grand visions. This, they think, is their chance to change the world or solve a problem that has bothered people for years! Then reality sets in and they accept that they are not going to be able to achieve this in 2,000, 6,000 or even 15,000 words. They get to grips with the difficult task of narrowing their focus on a piece of research that is manageable and feasible within the time limits set.

► In chemistry experiments you might choose a sample of a solution to test even though the word sampling may not be used for this.

You too will quickly realize that you cannot collect data from every member of the population you are interested in, whether this population is of people, animals, plants, towns, hospitals or whatever. You have to make a selection from that population. In other words you have to choose a sample. This is true whether you are observing, measuring, asking questions or collecting data in any other way. For example, if you are doing observation you may need to choose a sample of the possible **times** you are to observe, a sample of **places** you are going to observe, as well as a sample of **people** to observe.

IMPORTANT POINTS IN SELECTING A SAMPLE

Representativeness and generalization

► A representative sample can 'stand for' the wider population; this means that what you find out about the sample will probably be true of the wider population.

A piece of research becomes really valuable when the conclusions from it can be extended beyond the research. What this means is that what has been found out about a sample can be assumed to be true also of the population from which the sample comes. This means that the results are **generalizable**. For this to happen the sample must be large enough and must have similar characteristics to the population – in other words it must be 'representative'. You are already familiar with this idea in everyday terms. You are using it whenever you say: 'You can't generalize from that; it's not typical'.

When you don't need a representative sample

If someone were interested in how a particular decision was made by a local council, then the obvious selection of interviewees would be from those people who were closely involved in making the decision: councillors and local government officers. Here interviewees are 'expert witnesses' – although they are more usually called 'key informants' in research. If your research focuses on a particular event or process, then you will select interviewees for their inside knowledge. This kind of research does not require representativeness.

If someone were doing some research to see whether there was a demand for a fifteen-place playgroup in a local area, and received twenty positive replies, it might not matter much whether the researcher had polled a representative sample of parents: there are only fifteen places to fill. However, it might still be important to ensure that the fifteen represented an appropriate balance of male and female, working-class and middle-class, able-bodied and disabled, and white and black children.

Most student research, particularly in GNVQ assignments, involves studying one or two examples or 'cases', perhaps of workplaces or commercial organizations. Such **case studies** rarely include a representative sample, but you need to think of representativeness when choosing your case. Choosing a case study is dealt with later in this chapter (pp. 94–6).

The population you want to represent

Where samples are concerned, the term **population** is always used for the wider group the sample is supposed to represent – whether it is a population of people, places, times, trees or newspapers. You need to think carefully about this population when you are planning your research. Let's follow this through by playing with a project title.

> Title 1: To investigate the knowledge that parents in the UK have about their rights to choose a secondary school for their children, using personal interviews.

In this case 'population' is parents in the UK – all parents in the UK – and therefore the sample will have to represent this very large group. It will be impossible for a student researcher to interview a representative sample of parents, since it would be much too large and much too widespread.

> Title 2: To investigate the knowledge that parents **of children between 10 and 11 years old** in the UK have about their rights to choose a secondary school for their children, using personal interviews.

▶ If you need to select a representative sample, decide what population you want the sample to represent.

▶ **Population** is the general term for whatever it is that you want to generalize about. It might be a population of people living in a town, or of retail outlets, or of customers in a bank, or of words used in television advertisements.

The population is now parents of children in the UK who are at the point of selecting a secondary school. It is more feasible to select a representative sample of these, but still impossible for the student researcher to interview them all.

> Title 3: To investigate the knowledge that parents of children between 10 and 11 years old **in Patternbourne** have about their rights to choose a secondary school for their children, using personal interviews.

Now we have specified a geographical area. This not only reduces the size of the population, it also makes it more homogeneous because the population is a group of parents who, in theory at least, should all have access to the same information and all be covered by the same school selection procedures. It will be easier to select and to interview a representative sample of these parents. Any wider generalizations will, of course, depend on how representative Patternbourne is of other places.

> Title 4: To investigate the knowledge that parents with **a first child** aged between 10 and 11 years old in Patternbourne in 1994 have about their rights to choose a secondary school for their child, using personal interviews.

This title reduces the population even further and makes it more likely that a representative sample can be selected and interviewed. But this sample will be better for investigating certain things and worse for others. For example, if the interest was in the effectiveness of information given to parents, then it is an advantage to screen out the more knowledgeable parents who already have children at secondary school. But if the interest was in the factors that help parents to 'work the system', then screening out the more knowledgeable parents would not be a good idea.

How big is Patternbourne? If it is a town with a population of 80,000 people then there are likely to be more than 300 first-born children starting secondary school in September. If our student researcher is going to use an interview technique, then she will probably have time to conduct twenty interviews at the most. She will not be able to select twenty parents who will be fully representative of 300 parents. If she used a postal questionnaire she might gain information from more parents, but she would face all the problems associated with the fact that people often don't return postal questionnaires.

Our student researcher will now have to ask the question: 'representative in what ways?'

 Representative in what ways?

> Think about this question. What kind of diversity or variation among parents and children would this student researcher want to include in her sample of interviewees? Make a note of these variables.

Margin notes:

► A population is **homogeneous** if its units are similar to each other. If they are varied, the population is **heterogeneous**.

► A study of Patternbourne in 1994 might not produce valid generalizations for Patternbourne in 1984, or 2004.

► Populations need to be selected to fit the research question.

► On postal questionnaires see Chapter 5, p. 63.

We think that she would want to make sure that the parents of both male children and of female children were included in the sample, since parents may take more interest in the schooling of boys or girls. We also think that she would want to make sure that parents with different kinds of educational background and achievement were represented: it would be unrepresentative if the only interviews she did were with middle-class, professional parents. If she is interested in the effectiveness of the information given to parents, then she would probably want to include some parents whose first language was not English.

With only twenty interviews she won't be able to cover this diversity adequately, so her best bet is to select a sample that is representative in one or perhaps two of these ways in particular, and hope for the best about the others. Her project title might now be one of the following:

▶ What are the important diversities you want your sample to represent?

> Title 5: To investigate the knowledge that parents with a first child aged between 10 and 11 years old in Patternbourne in 1994 have about their rights to choose a secondary school for their child, using personal interviews with a sample representing the **parents of boys and the parents of girls.**

> Title 6: To investigate the knowledge that parents with a first child aged between 10 and 11 years old in Patternbourne in 1994 have about their rights to choose a secondary school for their child, using personal interviews with a sample representing parents **from different social classes**.

> Title 7: To investigate the knowledge that parents with a first child aged between 10 and 11 years old in Patternbourne in 1994 have about their rights to choose a secondary school for their child, using personal interviews with a sample representing parents **whose first language is English and parents whose first language is not English.**

Having solved one problem, our student researcher has now created other problems.

 Representative in one way and not representative in another

Suppose that our student researcher chose Title 5 and that her sample were composed as in Table 6.1.

Table 6.1 'Class' could be a confounding variable in this sample of parents of boys and parents of girls

	Parents of first-born boys	Parents of first-born girls	Total
Middle-class parents	8	3	11
Working-class parents	2	7	9
Total	10	10	20

Suppose that she finds that the parents of boys were much more knowledgeable about their rights than the parents of girls. What problem would she face in interpreting the results? Express this problem in your own words.

The problem is that, if our student researcher found that there were differences in the amount of knowledge between the parents of boys and the parents of girls, she couldn't be certain whether these differences were due to the gender of the children or to the fact that most of the parents of boys were middle class while most of the parents of girls were working class.

In this case our researcher would have done better to arrange a 5:5:5:5 sample (five middle-class boys, five middle-class girls, etc.) but five in each category would still be a very small number from which to draw conclusions.

HOW BIG SHOULD YOUR SAMPLE BE?

► If you are going to use statistical methods in your research, consult a statistician at an early stage.

► The greater the diversity that is to be represented, the bigger the sample has to be.

Statisticians have ways of calculating the minimum size of a sample that could adequately represent a population. The minimum size for a sample is not, in fact, determined by the size of the population, but by the amount of diversity you want the sample to represent.

The minimum size of a representative sample depends on the level of diversity you want it to represent

Think of four ordinary packs of cards all shuffled together. Think of yourself dealing them out. You know from a mixture of experience and common sense that you won't have to deal out very many cards before you get a sample that is roughly half reds and half blacks. If you are only interested in the red/black diversity of the population then a relatively small sample will be representative of this. In fact, if you dealt out ten cards there would be an 82 per cent chance that these would include no more than six blacks and no more than six reds. You will also know, intuitively, that if you wanted a representative sample of suits then you would need a bigger sample – there are four suits and only two colours, so the population is more diverse for suits than it is for colours. Again, if you wanted a representative sample of numbers, then you would need a bigger sample still, because there are thirteen different numbers in the pack.

Translated into the real world, then, a relatively small sample will be representative of gender in the population – so long as there are roughly 50 per cent males and 50 per cent females in the population – because there are only two genders. But a much larger sample would be required to be representative of age-groups in a neighbourhood. And the narrower the age groups you define, the bigger the sample would have to be.

You should now understand why researchers in a chemistry laboratory don't bother to say they are 'selecting a sample' of concentrated nitric acid. Concentrated nitric acid is always formulated in the same way. There is no diversity in the 'population' constituted by all the concentrated nitric acid in the bottle, or in the world: any one 'sample' of concentrated nitric acid is representative of all the others.

You will have to take advice from your tutor and other experts in deciding the size of your sample, but these are some of the implications of choosing a sample of a particular size:

- The smaller the sample, the less adequately it will represent diversity in the population.
- If your sample is smaller than twenty, it will be very difficult to do anything clever with statistics.
- Since the resources available to you are fixed, the larger your sample, the less you will be able to find out about each person, place or other unit in your sample.

The trade-off between breadth and depth

It is an iron law of research that with fixed time and resources you have to opt between finding out a little about many people, firms, nurseries, places, animals and so on, or finding out much more about very few. Thus, for example, a short questionnaire could be administered to a great many people, but it would yield only a little information about each of them; while a participant observation study could only focus on a few people or just one workplace, but might produce a great deal of information about each of them. Representativeness is relatively easy to achieve where a little is found out about many, and difficult to achieve where a lot is found out about a few.

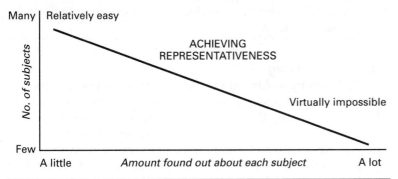

Figure 6.1 Graph illustrating the trade-off between breadth and depth in research

In the last resort your sample size will be determined by dividing the total amount of time and resources available to you, by the amount of attention you want to give to each item in the sample. For example:

► In making calculations like this, take into account the full 'cost' of each questionnaire or interview or observation; include the time to arrange, administer, transcribe, analyse and so on.

For a total time of 100 hours with 30 minutes for each questionnaire, the sample would be 200 (100 ÷ 0.5).

For a total time of 100 hours and 5 hours* for each interview, the sample would be 20 (100 ÷ 5).

(*15 minutes to arrange, 1 hour to travel and interview, 3¾ hours to transcribe and analyse)

TECHNIQUES FOR CHOOSING A SAMPLE

There are several methods for choosing a sample. We shall look at the main ones.

Probability sampling

The principle of probability sampling
The principle of probability sampling is that every member of the population should have an equal chance of being chosen as a member of the sample. Strictly speaking this means that in selecting a probability sample you need equal access to all members of the population: for example, a full listing of all the people admitted to a hospital over one year. There is not much point in selecting a probability sample if large numbers of those selected will be unavailable for studying.

Remember that the size of a representative sample is determined by the amount of diversity in the population you want to represent. In order to represent any degree of diversity, probability samples have to be large to allow the laws of chance to operate. Unless you only want to find out one or two things about the members of the sample, you probably won't be using probability sampling.

Probability sampling includes random sampling and systematic sampling.

Random sampling
We shall start by looking at the ideal situation. Suppose there is an opportunity to choose a large enough sample from a population. How do we choose the sample? To be truly representative, each item or person in the sample must have an equal chance of being chosen. One way to do this is to number the population and then to choose numbers at random. Some calculators have a random-number key, and tables of random numbers, generated by computer, are included in many statistics books.

If the population you are choosing from is relatively small, then you can make a random selection by putting numbered pieces of

► A random sample can only be properly drawn if the whole population is accessible. The list from which the sample is chosen is called a **sampling frame**.

paper or other objects representing each item in a bag and drawing items out for your sample.

> ### Random sampling with and without replacement
> To be truly random, each item should be replaced after selection. Suppose there are fifty items, then the first item out of the bag has a 1 in 50 chance of being chosen. If it is not replaced, then the next item has a 1 in 49 chance of being selected, and so on. However, if replacement means studying the same member of the population twice, this nicety is usually ignored.

Systematic sampling

Another method sometimes used for probability selection is to draw up a list of items in the population and then to go down the list selecting items in equal steps, such as every tenth item. This systematic sampling is only random if the population list was put together randomly in the first place. If it was put together in some other way, say alphabetically, then the selection is not truly random. However this is rarely an important consideration.

Stratified random sampling

In some cases you will know that your population consists of a number of significant groups. For example, if you were interested in the way that hospital staff communicate with patients you might wish to distinguish between 'care assistants', 'nurses' and 'ward managers'. Therefore you would wish to draw part of your sample at random from each of those groups. This is called stratified random sampling because in effect what you do is to divide your population into layers or 'strata' and choose a part of the sample from each layer.

Stratified sampling is sometimes used to solve the problem that in a random or systematic sample minorities may be poorly represented or not represented at all. Suppose, for example, a researcher wants to compare the leisure activities of the ethnic minority groups and the ethnic majority group of a community. Then the researcher might draw two random samples of the same size: one from the ethnic majority and one from among the ethnic minorities.

> ### The importance of the sampling frame in probability sampling
> You can only draw a good probability sample if you can arrange for every member in the population to have an equal chance of being chosen. Where the population is made up of places or objects, you will usually be able to construct a satisfactory sampling frame (such as all the farms in a county, or all large firms in a town). A sampling frame may not be so easily available when you are studying people. For example, if you are studying a local community and you start with the

▶ Ecologists, for example, investigating the distribution of plant species in an area of grassland using quadrats, can achieve random sampling by throwing the quadrat randomly over their shoulders. (Quadrat are sampling units of a known area, commonly 1 m² or 0.25 m², and they usually take the form of a square frame with wires fixed across.)

▶ **Systematic sampling** is another kind of probability sampling, where members of the sample are chosen in an arbitrary way that is unrelated to the main research interest. It is common practice for time sampling in observation studies where observations are made, say, every 12 minutes.

▶ In **stratified random sampling** the population is first divided into groups (strata) and then samples are drawn from each group.

telephone directory, you will under-represent people without phones, and ex-directory subscribers. If you start with the electoral register you will under-represent homeless people, newcomers to the area, and any people who are so suspicious of authority that they don't register. Sometimes this matters, and sometimes it doesn't. It will matter if the reasons why people aren't in the sampling frame – the list you start with – are relevant to your research project.

The non-response problem

In probability sampling the researcher takes a great deal of trouble to make sure that chance alone determines who or what gets into the sample. But that's only the first stage of the process. The researcher then has to find the chosen members, gain their cooperation and study them. Unfortunately, people or organizations do not necessarily make themselves unavailable or refuse to cooperate **at random**. A nicely drawn probability sample can turn into something that is not representative at all if the members who are chosen but not studied share some sort of distinction. Unless you know a great deal about the non-responders, non-response rates of more than 20 per cent usually undermine any generalizations that can be drawn.

Street surveys and probability sampling

Sometimes researchers who are studying people's attitudes or preferences try to choose random or systematic samples as they go along: for example, by selecting every fifth passer-by or using even less organized methods of selection. The population here is, of course, passers-by, at this point, during these times, on these days. The question is: 'How far is this population representative of any other population; what generalizations can be drawn from the sample?' This is a very poor way of drawing samples, and if you use it you should devise some means for working out how representative your sample turned out to be – see 'Representativeness in retrospect' later in this chapter (p. 95).

► In reality, the population in a street survey is likely to be passers-by, at this point, between these times, on these days, who looked as if they might answer questions and did in fact answer questions.

 Are you going to use a probability sampling technique?

You may know the answer to this question already, but even so check through the activity to make sure you have made the right decision.

	Yes	No
Are you going to collect only a little information from each member of the sample?	☐	☐
Can you afford to study a large sample?	☐	☐
Are you interested in only a few diversities in the population you are studying?	☐	☐
Is there a list, or could a list be made, from which you can select a probability sample?	☐	☐

If there is such a sampling frame, is it
complete and comprehensive in the ways
relevant to your research? ☐ ☐

Do you want to subject your data to analysis
using statistical tests? ☐ ☐

> ▶ For some kinds of research a map is a sampling frame. Clock-time is another kind of sampling frame.

In the activity above, the more yes boxes you tick the more appropriate probability sampling will be for you. You should nevertheless read on to see whether another technique might be preferable.

Quota sampling

Quota sampling is widely used in commercial research and opinion polling. It is much cheaper than probability sampling because representative samples can be composed with fewer people. You are more likely to find it useful for your purposes, especially if the population you are studying is composed of members of an organization that keeps good records about them.

Sample size

As with any other kind of sample, the ideal size will be determined by the amount of diversity you want to represent. For example, if you were taking a quota sample of a population of college students, then important categories might be:

18 and under/over 18

Male students/female students

Academic students/vocational students

That is $2 \times 2 \times 2 = 8$ quotas, each of which will need to be filled in proportion to the number of such students in the college. For example, if 15 per cent of students are mature, male, academic and full-time, then 15 per cent of your sample should be made up of students who meet these criteria. Ideally you need a minimum of five students in each quota so the total sample must be at least forty. Now try adding another category, for example, part-time/full-time. Now there are $2 \times 2 \times 2 \times 2 = 16$ quotas. To make sure you get at least five in each quota you will have to more than double the size of your sample – can you afford the time for this?

> ▶ In filling quotas, anyone who fits the criteria will do. Researchers often 'over-poll' and then delete any extras that they do not want. Much commercial street-survey work uses a quota technique and over-polling.

Using the quota principle more informally

To use quota sampling rigorously you need:

- good and relevant knowledge of the population from which you are drawing the sample;
- a big enough sample to enable you to represent different groups (quotas) in the proportions in which they occur in the population.

▶ The smaller your sample the fewer the quotas.

However, student researchers often find that they don't have the necessary knowledge or that they can't afford to take a big enough sample – or both.

All is not lost. First, so long as you make clear what you are doing you can make informed guesses about the population and build your quotas from these. Second, if you can't afford a sample big enough to represent the proportions in the quotas, you can still go ahead and fill the quotas with a number convenient to yourself. In the college example above, the researcher might have ignored the proportions in the population and instead opted to select five people for each quota. The sample would still be 'representative' but not in a proportional way: those from the largest categories would be under-represented, and those from the smallest categories over-represented. But it would still be possible to make sensible comparisons and contrasts between categories.

> ### Quotas in interview research
> If you are conducting interview research, doing twenty interviews or less, then the closest you will come to a representative sample will be through applying an informal quota technique. Choosing a small sample precisely to represent the important diversities in the population is a more reliable way of gaining representativeness than choosing a small sample at random.

▶ Where quotas are filled in a non-proportional way, there are techniques for weighting the results. Ask a specialist for advice about this.

 Are you going to use a quota sampling technique?

To help you decide, answer the following questions:

		Yes	No
1	Is probability sampling impossible for you?	☐	☐
2	Can you find out enough about the population to define the quotas – or at least make informed guesses about them?	☐	☐
3	Can you find out enough about prospective members to judge how they fit a quota?	☐	☐
4	Can you afford a sample large enough to fill each quota proportionately?	☐	☐

The more yes boxes you tick, the more appropriate quota sampling will be for you. But if your answer to 4 is 'no' then you have the option of reducing the number of quotas.

 Defining quotas

Only do this activity if you are seriously considering quota sampling.

Define the criteria for your quotas. Do this in the following way.

1 Define the important characteristics of your population. For example, in the case of a sample of firms, more than fifty employees/fewer than fifty employees, one location/several locations, etc.

2 Using your knowledge of the population, work out what percentage of the sample should fall into each quota.

3 Try to make the smallest quota contain five members, then work out the size of your sample. If that results in too large a sample, either reduce the number of quotas, or abandon the idea of filling the quotas proportionately.

Cluster sampling

It may be more convenient to select a particular group or groups within a population rather than selecting individuals. Thus a researcher might be interested in the childhood recollections of people over 75 years old. Even if a complete list of names and locations were available, it would be extremely difficult to attempt a random sample. But clusters of that age group exist in residential homes for the elderly. Thus a random sample of homes could be selected, and all the residents, or perhaps a random sample of them, could be interviewed.

▶ Ecological research nearly always involves **cluster sampling**. For example, fields may be chosen as 'clusters' and the plants within them sampled at random.

Opportunity sampling

If you are carrying out a fairly small project you will have limitations of time, finance and ability to travel. For these reasons you may be restricted to a sample that you can conveniently reach. You may have to rely entirely on the sample that is available to you. This is an opportunity sample.

▶ Opportunity sampling is also known as convenience sampling.

▶ See 'Representativeness in retrospect' later in the chapter (p. 95).

Snowball samples

A snowball sample is a particular kind of opportunity sample, used particularly in studying hard-to-reach groups. The researcher finds a first informant, interviews that person, and then asks for the names of other similar people. Then the interviewer repeats this procedure, and so on. Whether snowball samples are representative or not is always a puzzle. In some way, however, they are likely to be representative of networks of people, such as those with a particular leisure interest, and are probably the best way of studying networks.

▶ Snowball samples usually raise difficult issues about anonymity and confidentiality – see Chapter 2, pp. 8–9.

Connoisseur samples

A connoisseur is a well-informed judge of something. Occasionally researchers depend on judgements made by others. For example, a researcher wishes to investigate the characteristics of good managers. She selects a sample of companies and asks managers in those companies (her connoisseurs) to give her the names of people they consider to be 'good' managers. She then uses the recommended people as her sample. There are clearly some problems here, because different people will have different ideas about what constitutes a 'good' manager.

CASE STUDIES

Much student research is case study research, and this is positively encouraged in most GNVQ courses. In a case study, the researcher focuses on one or two people, or places or agencies. Sometimes research that uses a representative sample in one way is case study research in another. For example, you might choose a representative sample of customers of a tourist organization, but the organization itself will be a 'case', and your study would be a 'case study' of a particular organization. It will probably be something of a puzzle how far this particular organization represents other organizations even though you might have a sample of customers who are representative of this organization in particular.

The term 'case study' doesn't have any particular meaning and how you choose a case to study will depend on your overall research aims and on any limitations specified by your tutor or your syllabus. Here are some of the things you need to consider in choosing a case.

Key points in choosing a case to research

Research as the basis of generalizations

If your research is designed to use the particular – the case – to illustrate the general, then you will need to ask: 'How typical is this case?' For example, in childcare courses it is common for students to write a case study of a particular child. The child chosen doesn't have to be typical, but the student should be able to say how typical the child is. Similarly if the research were a case study of a particular motorway service station, then the student would need to be able to say how like and how unlike other service stations this one was. This has obvious implications for the data that needs to be collected.

Research to show your competence

In many health and social care courses the subject of the case study is not the client but the student. The case study is designed to give evidence of how well the student provided play opportunities for a child, helped a disabled person to dress, or something similar. Here the case or cases to choose are the ones that allow the student to show his or her competence best.

Alternatively, the research may be designed for the student to demonstrate his or her understanding of some aspect of the work, for example marketing. In this instance, the case or cases to choose

▶ Some research starts on the large scale, perhaps with a questionnaire, and then focuses down with a few case studies of whatever the questionnaire study showed to be typical.

are ones where you are sure you will have the cooperation of the marketing department.

Case studies chosen to be untypical

Sometimes the subject of a case study can be chosen precisely because it is untypical. For example, the evidence shows that female students are less likely than male students to study maths, physics or chemistry and that, when they do choose these subjects, they are in a small minority in their class groups. But much might be learned by making a case study of such students: what is it about them that they do not share with the majority of female students, and what is their experience of being in a minority in their classes? This is often called **deviant case analysis**.

Case studies as a starting point

Sometimes a case study of an unusual event is a good way of understanding what usually happens. For example, a researcher interested in an allotment society might choose to make a case study of a rare event, such as the large-scale vandalism of the allotments. How does this crisis illustrate the usual kinds of relationships between allotment holders? In a sense this is a 'naturally occurring experiment'. In choosing critical incidents for case-study treatment the usual question is: 'How much is this going to tell me about all the things that are usually taken for granted and not commented on?'

Practical considerations in choosing a case

The practical considerations involved in choosing a case depend very much on whether your research is **retrospective** or **prospective**.

Retrospective case studies

Retrospective case studies look at what has already happened. Choosing a case will include estimating how good people's memories will be, how good any written records are, and how cooperative the person or people featured in the case study are likely to be.

Prospective case studies

In opting for a prospective case study, you will be choosing a case now, which you will follow forwards into the future. You will have to speculate about the future. Will the people involved be around for the duration of your case study? Will they be cooperative for the duration? Will the kinds of things you want to study actually happen to them in the future?

The problem of access

Whether your study is retrospective or prospective, it will get nowhere unless you have access to the people, the situations and perhaps the records. Always remember that many aspects of the

► Where case studies are chosen to be untypical, this is called **deviant case analysis**.

► Analysing rare events can reveal a lot about how things normally function. This sort of study is called **critical incident analysis**.

► Most case studies are both retrospective – with a case history section – and prospective.

work of companies and organizations are, quite rightly, confidential. No firm is going to give you details of its marketing plans for the future; very few will give you access to its accounts. No social work agency should give you access to records; few will allow you to sit in on case conferences.

Hedging your bets in prospective case study research

If you are going to conduct a prospective case study consider whether you need to hedge your bets by embarking on more case studies than you actually need, to cover the risk of one or more of them collapsing on you.

 Choosing case studies

Do this activity if you are using a case study method.

	Yes	No

1 What is the case study supposed to stand for?

(a) Something typical? ☐ ☐

If 'yes', what is typical in the population of which this case is a member?

(b) Something untypical but illustrative of what is typical? ☐ ☐

If 'yes', what kind of unusual case do you need in order to illustrate the typical?

(c) Your own competence? ☐ ☐

If 'yes', then what characteristics does the case need to give you the maximum opportunities for showing your competence?

2 Is retrospective information important? ☐ ☐

If 'yes', what are you looking for in order to collect information from the past?

3 Is prospective information important? ☐ ☐

If 'yes', how will you choose a case to ensure that you can go on studying it for the duration of your project?

REPRESENTATIVENESS IN RETROSPECT

It is often not possible for a student, or even for a professional researcher, to achieve a fully representative sample. It is even more difficult to choose a 'typical' case to study. However, it may be possible to check in what ways the sample or case is unrepresentative. Often researchers collect information precisely for this purpose. For example, a researcher may not be particularly interested in the gender of his or her respondents, but may still record this. If the researcher knows that the population of interest is 60 per cent female and 40 per cent male, then the researcher will know that a representative sample should also show these proportions. If it does not, then the researcher should draw readers' attention to the fact that the sample is not entirely representative, and take it into consideration in drawing general conclusions from the research. For example:

> 'The sample under-represented part-time employees at the supermarket, so that generalizations about their opinions are made with less confidence than generalizations about the opinions of full-time employees.'

Similarly, a researcher might write:

> 'The tourist attraction studied may not be typical of others of its type since it has only been open for eighteen months. A repeat study in three years may reveal different results.'

Markers of representativeness

Whatever kind of sample you are using (but particularly if you are using a convenience sample, a cluster sample, a street survey, an informal quota technique, a probability sample that will have a poor response rate, or a case study approach), try to identify some aspects of representativeness with which you might assess how far your sample or case was, or was not, representative. You will need to find some information about the population that you can also easily find out about your sample. The more relevant this information is to your research question the better. Include this among the information you collect about your sample or case.

▶ You may not be able to select a fully representative sample or choose a typical case, but you should be able to identify and discuss the ways in which your sample or case is not representative.

Remember
In student research, few marks are allocated for the importance of your findings. Rather more marks are awarded for the quality of your research design. *Many* marks are allocated for showing what you have learned from doing the research. Showing that you understand the way your sample or case

turned out to be unrepresentative is one way of showing what you have learned.

CHAPTER SUMMARY

This chapter has been about choosing samples or cases for study. We have explained:

- when samples should be chosen to be representative, or cases to be typical – this is when you want to make generalizations from your research;
- the considerations involved in deciding on a sample size – the most important of these for you are likely to be time and money;
- various techniques for selecting samples, including probability sampling (random and systematic), stratified probability sampling, quota sampling, cluster sampling, opportunity sampling and connoisseur sampling;
- what you must consider when choosing cases for case studies;
- how to check whether your sample or case was indeed representative and in what ways.

You should now have a fairly clear idea about the way in which you are going to select the people, places, animals, organizations, newspapers, or whatever, that are going to feature in your research.

Making a time and action plan

Chapter objectives

After working through this chapter you will be able to:

▪ understand why it is important to identify the component tasks of your project;

▪ decide what priority each task has;

▪ estimate how long each task will take;

▪ draw up a time and action plan.

THE IMPORTANCE OF PLANNING

Once you have the beginning of an idea of what your research project is going to be about, you will be tempted to get started on it as soon as possible. Resist the temptation at all costs! It is far better to wait until you have drawn up a detailed time and action plan. This will ensure that you won't forget what to do and in what order, and it will also make sure that you know when you have to carry out certain tasks as well as any other fixed dates in the research programme. If you are working in a team, as will often be the case in GNVQ assignments, it is essential to make a plan, with each individual's jobs and deadlines clearly stated.

However large or small your research project is going to be, time spent planning it is time saved worrying about things later on. You can think about this planning stage as the equivalent of building foundations. No one would dream of building anything from a garage to a skyscraper without first building the foundations, because the strength of the foundations determines whether the building will stand up. So it is with planning research projects. Plans, like the foundations of buildings, can't be seen but the success of the research project depends upon them.

Having encouraged you to resist the temptation to rush straight into your project, let us work through the planning stages of a research project.

We shall assume that you have read all the preceding chapters about selecting your title and deciding on your methods, and that you have made a comprehensive resource statement.

The first task is to write out the title of your research project in full. The next thing to establish is what has to be done, by when it has to be done and, in the case of a team, who will do it.

This chapter will take you through the following stages:

▶ If you are doing a GNVQ course, make sure that you are familiar with the 'grading criteria', especially those concerned with planning.

▶ Scan through Chapter 13 on what to do when things go wrong. Good planning now will avoid some of these problems later.

▶ Research projects have a Quarter Rule, that is ¼ planning, ¼ carrying out, ¼ analysing, ¼ writing up.

- analysing your title,
- identifying all the tasks,
- putting the tasks in time order,
- estimating the time needed for each,
- identifying fixed dates,
- drawing up a time and action plan.

AN EXAMPLE OF PROJECT PLANNING

To enable you to see how this works in practice, we shall work through an example of a research project.

Let us take the title:

> Investigate the numbers and types of vehicles using the eastbound carriageway of the Orwell Bridge between 0800 and 0915 on weekday mornings in June, in order to recommend changes in the phasing of the traffic lights in the morning rush-hour.

You will need to have completed, analysed and written up your findings about traffic volumes before going on to the next stage of the project, which is to propose changes to traffic lights. It is very important that you complete the first stage of the project in sufficient time to enable you to undertake the second stage. You have also built a time element into your title, that is, between 0800 and 0915 on weekday mornings in June.

Having identified specific times and days when you will be undertaking your project, you must stick to them. Working through the time and action plan and planning the stages will help you to identify whether you will be able to undertake the research in the time available. If you discover that this is impossible, then you must amend the title.

Analyse the title and identify the tasks

Let us return to our example. We have chosen the command word 'investigate', but how exactly are we going to do this? In this example, we are going to stand at a safe distance from the edge of the road and in some way record the numbers and types of vehicles that use the eastbound carriageway of the Orwell Bridge between 0800 and 0915 every weekday morning during June.

 Identify the tasks

> Identify all the separate tasks you will have to do in order to 'investigate' as required in this example. What actions will you have to take?

We expect you identified some of the following:

- seeking advice from someone in authority about the safest place to stand to record the information;

- finding someone to accompany you, since undertaking this task on your own could be dangerous;
- making sure that you can get to and from the recording site every weekday morning in June;
- making sure that you would be excused from any other commitments you may have at these times;
- making sure that you had suitable clothing for all likely weather conditions;
- getting a letter from someone in authority in your school or college giving permission for you to undertake this assignment;
- devising a recording system, copying enough recording sheets and obtaining clipboards and pens or pencils.

You will probably have thought of other tasks, but the above list highlights that, for even the seemingly most simple project, a great deal of thought and planning is needed. This planning takes a considerable amount of time.

► Never underestimate how long simple organizational tasks can take.

So, from the one word 'investigate' we have identified a number of separate tasks that need to be undertaken, each of which take different amounts of time, and some of which have to be undertaken before others.

Put the tasks in time order

In the above list of some of the tasks involved in our investigation, which task do you think has to come first? We would say the highest priority is the seeking of permission to be absent from other commitments, as without this permission the rest of the project could not be undertaken. Perhaps the lowest priority is obtaining writing materials as these are easy and quick to obtain.

► Once you have a completed time and action plan you will probably find it helpful to make weekly 'do it' lists, saying what you (or each member of the team) have to do within the next few days.

When we prioritize tasks we are identifying which tasks need to be done before others. For example, obtaining permission to be absent from other commitments is essential before continuing with more detailed planning. Devising a recording system is another high priority task, which has to allow for the need to try out the recording system well before the first weekday morning in June.

Estimate the time needed

Having prioritized the tasks, we need to estimate how long each one of them will take. It is very easy to underestimate how long it will take to complete each task. For example, ensuring that you have suitable clothing for all likely weather conditions may only involve checking in the cupboard under the stairs for your raincoat, or arranging to borrow one, or going to the bother and expense of buying one.

► We have entered estimated times on the time and action sheet for this example.

While you are undertaking your project, you should enter the actual time taken for each task next to the estimated time. This normally makes for a few surprises. Some of your estimates will be fairly accurate, and some will be wildly out. We remember one student who estimated fifteen minutes to check a point in a book in the library. She actually took four and a half hours! She became so engrossed in the book that she forgot the time.

Table 7.1 A time and action plan for a project investigating traffic flow across the Orwell Bridge. (Note: For brevity, we have reduced the number of tasks in the plan.)

Task	Person respons- ible	Est. time* (hours)	Actual time (hours)	May 8–14	May 15–21	May 22–28	May 29– June 4	June 5–11	June 12–18
Write for permissions (maybe write a reminder)		2							
Visit site; identify place to stand		2							
Devise recording system		3							
Pilot and improve recording system		3							
Photocopy recording system		1							
Arrange transport to and from site		1							
Check suitable clothing		½							
Prepare and hand in synopsis of project		3							
Obtain writing materials		½							
Undertake observations		1¼ daily							
Make daily transcriptions of collected data		½ daily							
Prepare for oral presentation of project		6							
Oral presentation		1							
Analyse and write up		8							
Hand in project									

► If you are following a business studies course you can use your project work to demonstrate your management skills and your teamwork skills – but only if you record them.

It is important to enter the actual time against the estimated time, as only by practice like this can we ever hope to be able to develop reasonably accurate time-estimating skills, and therefore good time-management skills.

Identify fixed dates

► If yours is a group project then 'fixed dates' should include the dates for group planning meetings.

Now we need to identify any fixed dates, such as handing in a pre-liminary draft, giving an oral presentation about the project, leading a seminar, booking time to use a word processor and not forgetting the hand-in date. Don't forget the Quarter Rule,

¼ planning

¼ carrying out

¼ analysing

¼ writing up.

Draw up a time and action plan

By now you should have nearly all the information that you need to draw up the time and action plan. For the first draft of this you might like to use lining paper, flip-chart paper or even the back of an old roll of wallpaper. Whatever you choose, it must be large enough for you to have room for quite a lot of crossings out.

Later drafts can be much smaller and neater, and would ideally be no larger than two pieces of A4 paper taped together. This could be photocopied and one copy handed in with the project proposal, one copy kept pinned over wherever you do your studying, one copy kept stuck inside your project folder, one copy kept in your Record of Achievement to show as an example of your time-management skills, one copy to be included in the completed project, and one spare copy.

You may think this is a lot of copies, but it ensures that a copy is always available for you to keep a check on what tasks need to be done, when, and by whom.

When you have your entire project spread out before you and you can see at a glance what tasks have to be done and when, it saves you having to worry constantly about what should be happening. If you are in doubt, you only have to check your time plan. The time plan should also ensure that you complete your project within the time allowed. This is especially important if there are assessment criteria for planning, for time management, and for teamwork, as there are in the grading criteria used in GNVQ courses.

 Your own time and action plan

Draw up a first draft of the time and action plan for your own project. If this takes less than two hours, then either you have already done a great deal of planning, or you are not planning thoroughly enough. It might take a great deal longer. Even a short assignment requires a time and action plan.

▶ In drawing up your plan refer to:
- your listing of project management considerations;
- your resource statement;
(both of which you drew up when reading Chapter 3)
- your code of conduct (which you began in Chapter 2 and developed in Chapter 5).

CHAPTER SUMMARY

In this chapter we have shown you a way of making a time and action plan for your project. This means going through the following steps:

1 analyse your title,
2 identify all the tasks,
3 put the tasks in time order,
4 estimate the time needed,
5 identify fixed dates,
6 draw up time and action plan.

You will almost certainly have to revise your plan as you proceed, but it is easier to revise a well-made plan than to change ill-made plans in haphazard ways.

8 *Information from libraries*

ACCESS TO LIBRARIES

► Many college libraries are now called 'resource centres', reflecting the wide range of resources available. The activities in this chapter are all centred on libraries or resource centres and you will need access to a library to carry them out. Take this book to the library or resource centre and work on this chapter there.

► If you are doing a GNVQ course, make sure that you are familiar with the 'grading criteria', especially those concerned with information seeking and handling.

Whatever type of research you are engaged in, you will need to know where to find and how to access literature and other resources associated with your subject. Gathering information to support your findings and reading what other researchers have written are essential aspects of even a small-scale project. The most obvious place to look for this type of material is in the library. Although there are professional staff who can help you to locate material, the more independent a researcher you can become, the quicker you will be able to find information. The purpose of this chapter is to provide you with insights into the facilities, services and information retrieval systems you will find in libraries and resource centres. Many courses and qualifications, including GNVQs, will give you credit for skilful finding and handling of information. More particularly, skills in Information Technology (including the use of databases) are required for many qualifications, and are a core skill in GNVQ.

TYPES OF LIBRARY

Public libraries

Your local authority provides a library service that is free of charge. There is usually a large central reference library situated in the county town or city together with branch libraries in the suburbs and other small towns. Public library services sometimes operate mobile libraries that travel to outlying areas. It is generally advisable to consult your central library initially for research material and to find out the range of services that your library offers.

Academic libraries

As a registered student of an institution you are allowed access to the library of that institution. You will usually be able to borrow books and have full use of other library services. Most schools and colleges have qualified librarians to help you gain access to information. If you live near a university it is quite likely that you can obtain permission to use the library for reference, even if you are not a student there. However it is unlikely that you will be allowed to borrow books.

Specialist libraries

As you would expect, specialist libraries deal with particular subject areas. In addition there are specialist libraries that deal with information materials other than books, such as the British Film Institute which holds the national archive of films and film information.

Local record offices

County towns or cities will often have record offices containing the archives of local historical documents. These record offices sometimes hold archives of local newspapers.

► If you are a student, then the library you will use most will probably be the one based at your school or college. However, during the course of research, you will often need to call on a variety of sources and libraries. Advice on other libraries can be obtained from your school or college librarian.

> ### Training in library skills
> The larger and more complex the library, the more skilled you will need to be to find your way around. Library staff sometimes offer training courses, which are an excellent way of becoming familiar with the resources and services available to you.

 Access to libraries

Find out the address of your central public library, nearest branch library and local record office. Find out the opening times. Visit your central library, nearest branch library, local record office and college or school library. Do you need to be a member to borrow books? If so, then join. Is there a fixed loan period? If so, how is this depicted on the books? Is there a fines system? If so, how much? Does the library provide a guide for users? If so, get a copy. Find out what facilities these libraries offer and how they organize their resources. If this information is not in the library guide, ask a member of the library staff, with particular reference to your research interests.

TYPES OF MATERIAL FOUND IN LIBRARIES

Libraries don't just contain books. Most modern libraries see themselves as information resource centres and contain a wide selection of materials.

SUFFOLK COLLEGE LIBRARY GUIDE

Opening Hours

Termtime

Monday - Thursday	8.45am - 9.00pm
Friday	8.30am - 5.00pm
Saturday	9.00am - 12noon

Vacations

Monday - Thursday	9.00am - 5.00pm
Friday	9.00am - 4.45pm

LIBRARY LAYOUT

The Library holds over 60,000 books which may be borrowed by enrolled students. Some books are for reference use only within the Library and these are marked with a red band on the spine of the book.

Subject	Code Number
Computers	001
Psychology	150
Religion	200
Sociology	301
Economics	330
Law	340
Social Services	360
Education	370
Transport	385
Costume/Fashion	391
Languages	400
Mathematics	510
Physics	530
Chemistry	540
Medicine/Health	610
Nursing	610.73
Engineering	620
Motor Vehicles	629.2
Agriculture	630
Catering	640
Business	650
Management	658
Building	690
Art	700
Design	745.4
Music	780
Sport	796
Literature	800
Geography	910
History	940

The Audio-Visual (Resources) room is situated at the far end of the library.

Figure 8.1 Suffolk College library guide

▶ **Other library services:** Libraries often provide other facilities: coin- or card-operated photocopying and facilities for disabled people, such as text readers for the blind. Explore your own library and find out what facilities are available.

▶ When researching, **be creative**!

What's in the library?

Explore the library in the school or college where you are a student. Make a list of the range of resources it contains.

You may have found some or all of the following:

Books for reference and books for borrowing; text books and novels; academic studies; autobiographies and biographies; encyclopaedias; dictionaries; statistical information; bibliographies; indexes; abstracts; thesauruses; journals; cuttings; community information; government reports; local council reports; *Which* reports; periodicals; magazines; newspapers; journals; video tapes; audio tapes (for example, of music or oral histories); slides; plays; musical scores; records; paintings; maps; computer terminals; software packages; CD-ROMs. Some libraries also contain historical and archaeological artefacts, fossils and so on.

You may need to consult the standard text books on your research project, but your analysis will be enhanced by your undertaking wide research using the many resources available.

Identifying the kinds of resources needed

Write down the title of your project. Use a spidergram, like the one shown in Figure 8.2, to think through the types of library resources that would be useful to you.

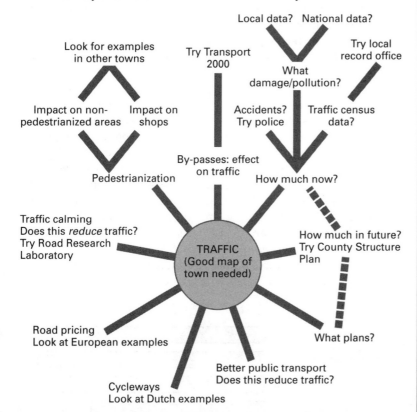

Figure 8.2 Spidergram showing the types of resources needed for a research project to: identify and discuss possible strategies for controlling the growth of traffic through the town centre

The subject heading of the project will influence the focus. Is it part of a Business Studies course, a Social Science course, an Environmental Science course, or what?

In a research project such as the one in our spidergram, the collection of primary data would be important. The title assumes that traffic is growing. This is a reasonable assumption but researchers must always find data to use as evidence, never relying on assumptions. You would therefore need to find out whether traffic was in fact growing, at what rate, why, and what hazards this produced. This would enable you to move on to discussing strategic responses to this problem. For this project it might be necessary to collect:

- data on traffic volume – for example, via a traffic survey;
- data on local opinion – for example, via interviews with motorists, pedestrians, local shopkeepers, the bus company, officials from the local council;
- data on accidents – from the police and the local authority.

For the book-based research, the student might need to study theoretical approaches in the social and environmental sciences, so that he or she could put the research into a wider theoretical context.

By consulting the local council's strategic plan, usually available in the central library, the student could find out the long-term projections for the growth of traffic and the council's strategies for controlling it. If this were a 'hot issue' there would be evidence of the debate in the records of the local council's meetings and in cuttings from the local newspaper, both available in central library or local record office.

To see how this debate compares to a wider discussion of the issues, the student could find out if there have been any recent articles in serious magazines such as *New Statesman and Society* and *The Spectator*, in specialist journals or in newspapers. It is important (unless you are carrying out a media research project) to use quality newspapers such as the *Guardian*, *The Independent* or *The Times*.

What about official statistics to compare with your local data? National statistics are collated and published by the Central Statistical Office. Three fascinating and useful digests of this type of statistical information are *Social Trends*, *Regional Trends* and the *General Household Survey* (all shelved at 312 under the Dewey system). Figure 8.3 and Table 8.1 are two pieces of information that we found in the 1993 *Social Trends* which would be of use in the project.

▶ Both the *Guardian* and *The Times* have an index that is found in most central libraries. Many resource centres will have this material on CD-ROM. Another useful resource for current affairs is *Keesing's Contemporary Archives*.

Figure 8.3 Households with regular use of a car: by socio-economic group[1], 1990

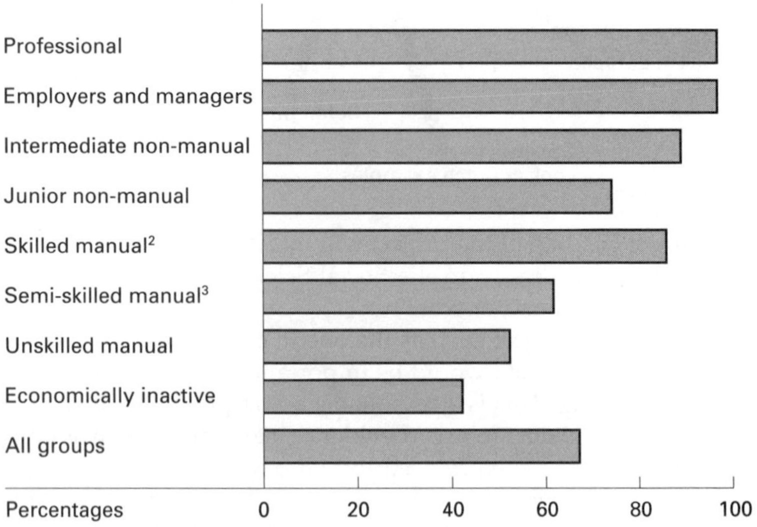

1   Excluding members of the Armed Forces, economically active full-time students and those who were unemployed and had never worked.
2   Includes foremen, farm managers and own account workers.
3   Includes personal service workers and farm workers.
Source: General Household Survey; Continuous Household Survey, Northern Ireland Office, © Crown copyright 1993. Reproduced in Social Trends 1993, HMSO, p. 183, 13.10.

▶ There may also be oral recollections recorded on audio or video tapes held by the central library.

▶ Never rely on one single source of information.

Historical comparisons of traffic growth might be part of the project. *Social Trends* can give a national historical comparison and the local record office may have information catalogued under 'traffic' that would be useful: for example, from old newspapers, previous council reports, or even grumbles from livery stables about the threat to their trade posed by motor cars at the beginning of the century.

Table 8.1 Cars[1] and car ownership: by region, 1981 and 1990

United Kingdom | | | | | | | Percentages and cars per 1,000 population
	1981				1990		
	Percentage of house-holds with-out the regular use of a car	Percentage of households with regular use of			Percentage of house-holds with-out the regular use of a car	Percentage of households with regular use of		
		One car only	Two or more cars	Cars per 1,000 pop.		One car only	Two or more cars	Cars per 1,000 pop.
Great Britain	40	45	15	281	33	44	23	363
North								
Yorkshire and Humberside	48	41	10	227	42	43	16	295
East Midlands	37	47	15	273	31	44	24	351
East Anglia	31	51	18	321	26	47	26	420
South East	36	46	19	316	28	44	28	396
Greater London	45	42	14	287	38	42	19	355
Rest of South East	30	48	22	336	23	45	32	420
South West	31	51	18	329	25	48	27	410
West Midlands	38	46	16	290	35	42	24	386
North West	45	42	13	250	37	44	20	338
England	39	45	16	288	32	44	23	372
Wales	38	47	15	271	30	49	21	346
Scotland	49	40	11	217	42	41	17	294
Northern Ireland	40	46	14	237	34	47	19	302

1 Includes cars and vans normally available to the household.
Source: Department of Transport. Reproduced in *Social Trends 1993*, HMSO, p. 183, 13.9.

If the college or school library has a video resource catalogue you may find that your topic has been investigated by current affairs programmes such as Panorama, or World in Action. Such programmes usually offer an accessible and well-researched point of view.

Don't take information at face value

With any information resource – newspapers, the minutes of local council meetings, government reports, television pro-grammes – it is important never to take them at face value. You should always read or view them critically, being aware that they may be biased or at least selective in the information they present. The wider you conduct your research, the more scope you will have to sample a range of opinions and angles on your subject and find evidence that you can use to form your own point of view.

FINDING YOUR WAY AROUND LIBRARIES

The range of information resources held by your local libraries is important to you as a researcher. How do you find your way around? How is the information organized?

Before you begin

Remember that although libraries are wonderful places, they are also places in which researchers can waste a great deal of time. Sometimes libraries can also induce panic in researchers who, once they become aware of the sheer scope and amount of information available, find it hard to discriminate between the essential and the peripheral and become anxious that they will 'miss' something.

To avoid wasting time in the library
1 Ensure that your research project is well focused and that you maintain that focus when searching for library information.
2 Ensure that you know how to find library information.

Classification of library books

Library books are usually arranged under subject headings. Exceptions to this are the quick reference section of the library (such as dictionaries, yearbooks, encyclopaedias, indexes and abstracts) and the fiction section, which is arranged alphabetically under author's surname. However, the scale and complexity of most libraries would make the simple ordering of books under broad subject headings rather meaningless. Most libraries use one of the standard classification systems for arranging the books and other resources that they store. The system you are most likely to find used in British libraries is the Dewey Decimal Classification System, although there are other systems such as the Bliss Bibliographic Classification or the Library of Congress Classification.

Dewey Decimal System

The Dewey system was invented by an American librarian, Melvil Dewey, in 1873 and is now in its twentieth edition. Within the Dewey system, broad subject areas are divided into ten classes, each of which is assigned a three-figure number:

Generalities	000–099
Philosophy and related disciplines	100–199
Religion	200–299
Social Sciences	300–399
Languages	400–499
Pure Sciences	500–599
Technology (Applied Sciences)	600–699
Arts (including Recreation)	700–799
Literature	800–899
Geography, Biography, History	900–999

Each of these main classes is then subdivided, for example:

Social sciences	**300**
Statistics	310
Political science	320
Economics	330

Law	340
Public Administration	350
Social Services	360
Education	370
Commerce, communication	380
Customs and folklore	390

The process of subdivision and increasingly specific classification of subject area is continued so that each of these classes is divided again, for example:

Customs and folklore	**390**
Costume and accessories	391
Public and social customs	394
Etiquette	395
Folklore	398

You may find that some books have very long Dewey numbers – don't let this bother you. The sophistication of the Dewey system allows for this increasing subdivision of subject area.

 Identifying the relevant code numbers

First check that the main library you will use uses the Dewey Decimal system. If it does, make a note of which Dewey classification numbers would be of most help to you in conducting your project. Then, using the library guide, find out where these numbers are shelved.

▶ If the library you use has a different system, find out about it from the library guide and carry out the same activity for this system

While you are at the shelves, make a note of some books that may be useful – note down the author, title, and Dewey number (found on the spine of the book).

Make a neat copy of the Dewey numbers most relevant to you, and keep this in the back of your diary or in your project file.

The library catalogue

The classification and the cataloguing of library books go together. Libraries have a catalogue that lists all the books within the stock of the library. This information used to be stored on library index cards, but most modern libraries have computerized library catalogues with each book listed under its **title**, its **author** and its **subject**. You can use the library catalogue to find out:

- if the library has a specific book (by title or author);
- what other books the library contains by a specific author;
- what books the library contains on a particular subject or combination of subject areas.

It is therefore very much in your interests to become familiar with the library catalogue – it will save you much time searching through the library shelves!

Although some people feel happier with 'hard copy' library systems, computerized systems, once you are used to them, are much faster and more comprehensive. Most computerized library catalogues have very clear user instructions – you don't have to be a computer expert. They are generally menu-based, and use on-screen instructions to guide you through the process of accessing the information you require. If you get stuck, ask a member of the library staff – they are there to help you.

 Using the library catalogue

Find the library catalogue for the library in which you usually work. Look up the entries for some of the books you listed earlier, using these different approaches:

1   by author's name,
2   by book title,
3   by subject.

What details were listed? The Dewey number will always be listed so that you can find the book on the library shelves, and some more sophisticated systems will provide the date of publication and the publisher. You will need this information in case the book you require is out on loan and you wish to reserve it.

 Further work on the library catalogue

Investigate what other books the author has written, and what other books the library has within the same subject area.

If you type in, say, 'pollution' as your subject area you will probably find that the computer traces far too many books to be of use to you. (The computer in our college library came up with 124 titles.) It is better to try to be more specific about the subject areas – sometimes combining two areas: for example, road transport (our computer found fifteen), air pollution (our computer found twenty-five) or urban environment (our computer found three) as follows:

Urban environment

Central Council for the Disabled	Planning for Disabled People in the Urban Environment	362.4
Merce C	Living in Cities, Psychology and the Urban Environment	301.36
Douglas I	Urban Environment	573.4

Accessing other library resources

We have already mentioned some other library resources you may find useful. Each library will organize these in its own particular way, so the following is offered as a general guide.

▶ With the increasing computerization of library catalogues, you may find that the catalogue can give you additional information, such as whether the book is out on loan; what type of loan it is held on (for example, short term); how many readers are waiting to borrow the book; a brief résumé of the content of the book; a list of other titles by the same author and so on.

Newspapers

Current newspapers are usually set aside in a reading area of the library. Because of the problem of storage, most libraries will not keep back copies for very long, although they may operate a newspaper cuttings service which would be indexed by subject.

Some libraries will have copies of quality newspapers on microfilm or microfiche. You will need to ask how to use a microfilm or a microfiche reader. The same applies to newspapers available on CD-ROM.

► It is possible to obtain copies of material stored on microfilm or microfiche.

Journals, magazines and periodicals

These publications will usually be arranged in a reading area of the library, often on separate shelving that allows the front cover of the publication to be displayed. Academic journals may be filed in magazine boxes in a separate section of the library in alphabetical order, perhaps with current copies displayed on the shelves. After a certain time the back copies are often bound into year books and these bound volumes will usually feature in the library catalogue.

Pamphlets

The distinction between a pamphlet and a book is not a clear one. Books are usually bound between covers, whereas pamphlets are often stapled or heat-sealed. Pamphlets are classified in the same way as books are – given a Dewey number, shelved in the appropriate place and appearing in the library catalogue. They are sometimes placed in a magazine box on the library shelves.

Maps

Because of their size, maps are often filed in special map-filing cabinets which allow them to be kept flat.

Video tapes, films, records, slides, audio tapes

If your library has an audio-visual section, this will often have its own catalogue. Many school and college libraries have such a section that contains audio and video tapes (both feature films and off-air recordings), records and photographic slides. There is usually a separate catalogue for such resources, sometimes filed under subject and/or using the Dewey classification system with a separate section for feature films. Not all libraries allow video or audio tapes to be borrowed. Instead there may be listening and viewing facilities within the library.

Computers and electronic databases

Many modern libraries have at least one computer terminal from which you can access huge amounts of information. It is usually sensible to ask a member of staff to introduce you to the system but, once this is done, you will find that it is very easy to search for information. In fact, the problem is usually that you find more information than you can handle. Selecting what is relevant is an important skill for which you will be rewarded in your assessment.

What if the book or journal I want is not on the shelf?

Check the library catalogue – does the library have a copy of the book you are seeking?

If the library does have a copy

If the book is in the library catalogue but is not on the shelf, it could be because it is:

- out on loan;
- being used somewhere in the library;
- awaiting re-shelving;
- on order;
- in another section (e.g. large books section, pamphlets section).

Check with the library staff – you will probably be able to reserve books that are out on loan. Find out from the library staff how you can reserve a book. Usually you need to complete a request card like the one shown in Figure 8.4.

► You will need to provide the following information:

Author
Title
Date of publication
Publisher
Source of information

SUFFOLK COLLEGE LIBRARY BOOK REQUEST/RESERVATION	Tel No: (01473) 296585 (Direct Line) or 255885 ext. 6585 In the event of any query this copy must be produced				
AUTHOR					
TITLE					
PUBLISHER		**YEAR**		**ISBN**	
REFERENCE SOURCE (eg Name of book)					
BORROWER'S NAME	**ADDRESS**				**TEL. NO.**
COURSE					
LIBRARY USE ONLY					
DATE		**SHELVES CHECKED**	**SOURCES CHECKED**	**FURTHER ACTION**	**DATE**
DYNIX					
DATE BOOK(S) FOUND IN ISSUE					

Figure 8.4 Suffolk College book request/reservation card

If the library doesn't have a copy

If the book is not listed in the library catalogue, you may be able to borrow it using the interlibrary loan service, whereby books can be borrowed from other libraries or from the British Library Lending Division. Modern libraries see themselves as part of a wide information network, and there will sometimes be arrangements between neighbouring local authority library services to borrow books from each other. Most libraries will also be able to borrow books nationally from the British Library Lending Division. This service is not free and you will be required to pay a fee.

Some libraries will also operate a service whereby you can obtain copies of journal articles from journals that the library doesn't hold. Once again, you will need to give precise information (see Figure 8.5).

SUFFOLK COLLEGE LIBRARY JOURNAL REQUEST	Tel No: (01473) 296585 (Direct Line) or 255885 ext. 6585 In the event of any query this copy must be produced

JOURNAL TITLE	
AUTHOR OF ARTICLE	
TITLE OF ARTICLE	

YEAR	VOL. NO.	PART	PAGES	BL NO ISSN

BORROWER'S NAME	ADDRESS		TEL. NO.
COURSE			

COPYRIGHT DECLARATION
I declare
 i) I have not already been supplied with a copy of this material by any Librarian.
 ii) I will use the copy only for the purposes of research and/or private study.
 iii) As far as I am aware, no other person with whom I work or study has made, or is likely to make,
   a request for the same material.
   Signed   Date

SOURCE	LOCATION	DATE SENT	DATE REC'D	N/A RET'D		
SUUS						
EULOS						
BLDSC	ARTTEL NO.				WLIST	BACKUP
OTHER						

▶ You will need to provide the following information:
Author
Title of article
Title of periodical
Number, part and date of volume
Page reference

Figure 8.5 Suffolk College journal request and photocopy declaration card

SEARCHING FOR INFORMATION

Earlier, we mentioned the quick reference section of the library. Here you will find general reference books that can be of considerable help to you, particularly in the early stages of research or if you wish to clarify information about a topic.

Quick reference books

 Exploring the quick reference books

For your own project explore the quick reference books to see where you would find:

(a) definitions of key terms (often one of the first tasks involved in carrying out a research topic is to define precisely the terms that you use);
(b) information on an eminent person important to your topic.

Dictionaries

Most libraries will stock one or two sets of a good dictionary, such as *The Oxford English Dictionary* or *Collins English Dictionary*, which will provide short definitions of terms. There are other dictionaries that might be useful in the course of your research, such as *The Oxford Dictionary of Modern Slang* or *The Oxford Dictionary of Quotations*, or specialist dictionaries such as *Collins Dictionary of Business*.

If you are searching for a word for your essay, you will find help in *Roget's Thesaurus*. Roget lists commonly used words and offers a number of other words that have a similar meaning, as well as words that mean the opposite. There is also the *Collins Paperback Thesaurus in A–Z Form*, which can be bought in combination with the *Collins English Dictionary*. Major word-processing packages such as Word and WordPerfect include a thesaurus as well as a program that checks spelling.

Encyclopaedias

Encyclopaedias provide detailed summaries of current knowledge about particular topics. They are organized in alphabetical order. The *Encyclopaedia Britannica* and *Chambers Encyclopaedia*, both multi-volume sets, are found in most libraries. Several major encyclopaedias, including *Hutchinson's*, *Grolier* and *Encarta* are available on CD-ROM.

Whitaker's Almanac, although not an encyclopaedia, is a very useful source of information about Britain and the rest of the world. The focus is on current affairs, education, social services, institutions, government and so on.

Biographical information

Information on eminent people can be found in *Who's Who*, in *Who Was Who* (which contains the biographies of people who were in *Who's Who* and who are now dead) and *Who Owns Whom*, a list of business ownership. There is also the *Dictionary of National Biography*, which contains information about famous people.

Information on current events

Keesing's Contemporary Archives is a weekly digest of major world events. It is compiled by summarizing information in official reports, serious newspapers and magazines.

Abstracts and bibliographies

There are also books that are lists of books. Abstracts give short summaries of books and articles. Bibliographies give lists of books and articles under particular subject headings – usually with a few notes about them. There may be abstracts or bibliographies for your research subject area. Use the library catalogue to find out. This is dealt with further on pp. 164–5.

Compiling a reading list

If you are devising your own research project or if you have been given a basic reading list that needs to be supplemented, you will need to find out what other books and articles have been written on your subject area. A reading list should be as up to date as possible. The first place to consult is the catalogue of your library. Make a note of any books that look relevant and then check out the book. If you make use of it, add it to your list.

The next place to look for possible sources is in one of the major

► When you include a reading list in your project report it should consist of books you have actually referred to.

► See Chapter 9 on note-taking.

bibliographies, such as the *British National Bibliography*. *British Books in Print* and *Whitaker's Book Bank* list all books currently in print in Britain. However these don't tell you what the books are about, so see if there is a specialist bibliography or volume of abstracts for your subject area first.

Check which of these bibliographies is available in your library. If you find books in these listings that your library does not stock and that may be of use, you can request a copy on interlibrary loan.

Information on articles published in journals and periodicals is available in indexes and abstracts. These are compilations of articles on topics that have appeared in academic and professional publications. They are arranged under subject and topic headings. Abstracts will also provide a brief summary of the article. *The British Humanities Index*, the *British Technology Index*, *The Art Index* and *ASSIA – Applied Social Science Index of Abstracts* are examples. Indexes and abstracts usually appear three to six months after the periodicals they cover.

Another source of good, up-to-date information is provided by newspaper indexes such as *The Times Index*. This digest contains a compilation of articles from *The Times* newspaper arranged under topic heading. Another listing of newspaper articles is the *Clover Newspaper Index*, which is arranged in subject/topic headings and gives details of articles that have appeared on each topic in the quality newspapers.

Electronic sources

It is becoming increasingly common for certain types of library information, particularly information that needs to be as up to date as possible, to be available on CD-ROM (compact disc, read only memory) or through on-line computer searches. The use of CD-ROMs will usually be free (although you may have to pay for printouts) and easy to use (ask library staff for an introduction), whereas on-line computer searches will usually entail a small charge.

▶ Remember that information technology is now a required core skill in many courses, especially vocational courses such as GNVQ.

There has been a very rapid increase in the number of CD-ROMs published in the last two years. They contain a wide variety of information, including:

- standards information – information on British and international standards;
- occupational health and safety (OSH) databases – covering mainly journal articles and pamphlets;
- *Whitaker's Book Bank* – a complete record of all British books in print, forthcoming books and books recently out of print.

In addition there are many CD-ROMs that contain encyclopaedias, dictionaries, *The Times Index*, *The Times 2000* (information about the major companies in the world), *The Times World Atlas and Database*, and many more.

▶ There may be a charge for an on-line search.

▶ There are many more databases in addition to those listed here, and since computerized storage of information is a growth area, it is worth checking individual libraries for details of which databases and CD-ROMs they have.

▶ If the first key word doesn't pay off, try another, and another, and another.

On-line computer searching

Commonly found computer databases include:

- BLAISE (British Library Automated Information System), which covers mainly British book material on all subjects, but also includes conference reports, theses, music and audio-visual material;
- DIALOG, an American system holding over 300 databases, which concentrate on journal articles in all subject areas;
- Eurobases, a series of databases held by the European Commission, including a database called Cellex, which covers information on European law.

Searching a database

 A book search

Carry out a search using *British Books in Print*, *British National Bibliography* or *Whitaker's Book Bank* to find additional books for your project. Try using different subject names or combinations.

One of the skills of searching is to refine your search continually in the light of the information you retrieve. When we tried a search for the traffic growth project we found that 'pollution' did not yield much useful material.

You need to think creatively of other words that might trigger useful data. In our example, these might be 'air pollution', 'road traffic pollution', 'urban pollution' or 'environmental hazards'.

We typed 'urban environment' into the CD-ROM of *Whitaker's Book Bank*, which yielded twenty-eight titles. Some could be discarded as irrelevant (*Earthquakes and the Urban Environment*), or too old (1969), or too specialist (*Cold-formed Steel for Tall Buildings*). From this initial sift, we were left with eight possible titles, which we called up in more detail. We eventually found one book that could be of use, although it is an American publication and the findings might not be relevant to the task.

 A search using indexes and abstracts

Try the same exercise using the same and other key words with indexes, abstracts and general reference books. If they are available, search specialist bibliographies.

CHAPTER SUMMARY

This chapter has outlined:

- the types of facilities and information contained in libraries and resource centres;

- the ways you can go about retrieving information from a library to compile a reading list.

You have worked through this chapter once, but you may need to regard it as a reference section to return to again.

Once you have found what you want in the library you will need to read, view or listen to it and make notes. There is advice on this in Chapter 9.

9

Reading, making notes and keeping records

► This chapter introduces you to the skills of reading, making notes, and filing and retrieving data. These are essential skills for anyone undertaking research, whether it is descriptive or explanatory. The chapter refers mainly to books, but remember there are other sources that might be relevant to you. (See Chapter 8 for some ideas about other sources.)

Chapter objectives
After working through this chapter you will be able to:

▮ preview printed material to assess its relevance to your research task;

▮ read widely and selectively, to gather a variety of data related to your research task;

▮ read intensively to explore a particular issue in detail;

▮ make notes of what you have read;

▮ file and retrieve notes and other data.

PREVIEWING READING MATERIAL

► This stage of research is called a 'literature search'.

Any research project, however small, usually involves reading what other people have written about your area of interest. If you have been given a topic for investigation, it is likely that you have also been provided with a list of books and articles as 'recommended reading'. This list is your starting point and should provide a useful introduction to the subject area and pointers to further reading. If you are not given a recommended reading list, or if you wish to pursue a line of enquiry beyond your introductory reading, you will have to search out and preview written material for its relevance to your task (see Chapter 8: Information from libraries).

Being able to preview a book for its relevance to your research task is a valuable skill because it can save you a great deal of time. The first step is to familiarize yourself with what a book contains. The following section provides an outline of the components of a book. Under each heading we suggest questions you might ask yourself when assessing whether a book will be useful for your purpose.

The components of a book and the questions you should ask

Title
• What does the title of the book tell you about the content?

Cover
• What information does the cover of the book give you about the contents and the author?

The 'blurb' on the cover can often give you a short summary of the book and an early indication of its use to you.

Author/editor

- Is there any information about the author/editor that gives you an indication of his or her experience and standing in the subject, such as details of posts held or previous publications?
- Have you heard of the author before or read anything else written by him or her?

Date and place of publication

- When was the book first published?
- Where was it published?
- Has it been reprinted?
- Has it been published in second or later editions?
- What is the publication date of your copy of the book?

The answers to these questions will indicate how recent the book is, whether it has sold enough copies to be reprinted, and in which countries the book has been published. As a general rule, it is a good idea to read the most up-to-date books you can find on your subject, as these should reflect current findings and thinking while recognizing and building upon previous knowledge.

Publisher

- Who published the book?

You will need to give this information, together with details of the author, title, place and date of publication, in any references you make to the book when writing up your research (see pp. 164–5).

Table of contents

- Is the table of contents detailed enough to help you decide whether the book is relevant to your enquiries? If not, you will have to look in more detail at the contents themselves.
- Are all or part of the contents relevant to your research task and other material you may have read?
- Do any of the sections appear familiar or especially interesting?

Foreword, Preface or Introduction

- If the book has a foreword, preface or introduction, does it tell you about the content of the book, why it has been written and who the intended audience is?
- Is the foreword written by the author or by someone else?

Text

- Is the text a primary or a secondary source?
- Can you identify an introduction and a conclusion to the book?

▶ **Primary** and **secondary** sources are explained later in this chapter, pp. 126–7.

- Are there outlines of chapter content, or subheadings to guide you in your reading of the book, or a clear conclusion?

Layout/illustrations
- Are there any diagrams, graphs, tables, photographs, etc., that are helpful and easy to understand?
- Do you find the printing style and design of the pages easy to read?

Glossary
- Does the book have a glossary of the specialist words and terms it uses?
- If so, how many are already familiar to you?
- Are the explanations and definitions clear?

Bibliography and references
- Does the book have a bibliography or a references section? Strictly speaking, a bibliography is a list of all publications that the author has consulted in writing the book, whereas a references section lists only those sources referred to or quoted from in the text. (See Chapter 11, p. 164.) Most academic textbooks have one or the other, with a system of referring to works either by notes (footnotes or endnotes) or using the Harvard author-date system. A bibliography can be a useful indicator of further reading on or around your research topic.
- How recent are the published sources referred to in the bibliography or references section?

Index
- Does the book have an index?
- If so, what does it tell you about the contents of the book?
- Is more weight given to some subject areas than others?

A quick glance through an index can tell you the major areas covered by the book.

Looking at a book

When previewing a book, the order in which you ask the above questions depends on your preference. Some people plunge straight into the text to see what they can learn about the content and the author's style. Others prefer to look at the information that surrounds the text such as the index or the publication details.

Imagine you are previewing a book to evaluate its usefulness for a project. What could you learn from different features of the book? We shall take as an example a book called *Come On Down?*, used for a project on the characterization of women in soap operas.

Title page

Come On Down?

Popular media culture in post-war Britain

Edited by
Dominic Strinati
and
Stephen Wagg

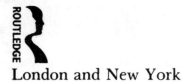

London and New York

Figure 9.1 The title page

The title Come On Down?, reflecting a catchphrase from a well-known television show, immediately links the book to popular culture. The subtitle explains more precisely the focus of the work. It is common for academic texts to use the subtitle to clarify content in this way.

▶ Subtitles are often a helpful guide to the contents of a book or article.

The editors are given prominence, which alerts the reader to the fact that the book is a collection of the work of several contributors.

The cover 'blurb'

Figure 9.2 The cover 'blurb': a quick indication of the book's contents

▶ Remember that most of the 'blurb' is advertising copy, written to sell the book. Books sometimes do not live up to the advertising claims.

The 'blurb' on the back is most useful, stating succinctly what the book is about and identifying television soaps as one of the areas covered.

An instant guide to the subject content is given in the single line towards the bottom of the cover giving a library-style classification:

> 'Cultural studies/media and communication studies'

Forewords and prefaces

This book has a foreword – although it is not named as such. In this case it is an expanded version of the cover 'blurb' and gives more information about the editors.

Come On Down?

Come On Down? presents an introduction to popular media culture in Britain since 1945. It discusses the ways in which popular culture can be studied, understood and appreciated, and covers some of its most important forms and processes, and the key analytical issues they raise.

The contributors analyse some of popular culture's leading and most representative expressions: TV soaps, quizzes and game shows, TV for children, media treatment of the monarchy, pop music, comedy, advertising, consumerism and Americanization. The diversity of both subject-matter and argument is the most distinctive feature of the collection, making it a much-needed and extremely accessible, interdisciplinary introduction to the study of popular media culture.

The contributors, many of them leading figures in their respective areas of study, represent a number of different approaches which themselves reflect the diversity and promise of contemporary theoretical debates. Their studies encompass issues such as the economics of popular culture, its textual complexity and its interpretations by audiences, as well as concepts such as ideology, material culture and postmodernism.

The editors: Dominic Strinati is a lecturer in sociology at the University of Leicester. His previous work has been in the areas of political and industrial sociology, and he is the author of *Capitalism, the State, and Industrial Relations* (1982). He is currently working on a book on theories of popular culture. Stephen Wagg has taught sociology in further, higher and adult education since the mid-1970s and is currently tutor in sociology at the University of Leicester. He wrote *The Football World* (1984) and, with John Williams, edited *British Football and Social Change* (1991). He occasionally organizes and compères comedy shows.

Figure 9.3 The foreword to the book

Imprint page

The publisher's information on the imprint page shows that this is a fairly recent publication (1992) which promises up-to-date contributions. It also includes the ISBN number, which you would use if you wanted to order your own copy from a bookshop, and it

▶ On preparing bibliographies and references sections, see Chapter 11, pp. 164–5.

includes most of the information you need to write an entry for the book in the bibliography or references section of your project.

First published 1992
by Routledge
11 New Fetter Lane, London EC4P 4EE

Simultaneously published in the USA and Canada
by Routledge
a division of Routledge, Chapman and Hall, Inc.
29 West 35th Street, New York, NY 10001

This collection © 1992 Routledge; individual chapters © 1992 individual contributors

Typeset in 10 on 12 point Baskerville by
Witwell Ltd
Printed in Great Britain by
T.J. Press (Padstow) Ltd, Padstow, Cornwall.

All rights reserved. No part of this book may be reprinted or reproduced or utilized in any form or by any electronic, mechanical, or other means, now know or hereafter invented, including photocopying and recording, or in any information storage or retrieval system, without permission in writing from the publishers.

British Library Cataloguing in Publication Data
Come on down?: popular media culture
  in post-war Britain.
  I. Strinati, Dominic
  302.2373

Library of Congress Cataloging in Publication Data
is also available

ISBN 0-415-06326-4
        0-415-06327-2 (pbk)

Figure 9.4 The imprint page

Contents page

You will see that Chapter 5, 'British Soaps in the 1980s', looks the most useful for this project. We would also consider Chapter 4, and perhaps scan the beginnings and ends of the other chapters and look at their references/bibliographies.

Contents

Figure 9.5 The contents page

References

The references at the end of Chapter 5 give some extremely useful
pointers to further reading. In particular, Geraghty's book *Women
and Soap Opera* looks worth following up for this project.

▶ References are sometimes given
at the end of chapters, and
sometimes at the end of books.
Sometimes the references (works
the author referred to) are
supplemented by a separate
bibliography (works the author
recommends you to read).

REFERENCES

Brunsdon, Charlotte (1981) '*Crossroads*: notes on soap opera', *Screen* 22(4).

Buckingham, David (1987) *Public Secrets*, London: British Film Institute.

Dyer, Richard (ed.) (1981) *Coronation Street*, TV Monograph 13, London: British Film Institute.

Geraghty, Christine (1991) *Women and Soap Opera*, Oxford: Polity Press/Basil Blackwell.

Modleski, Tania (1982) *Loving with a Vengeance*, London: Methuen.

Nursing Times 84(26), 29 June.

Redmond, Phil (1987) *Phil Redmond's Brookside: The Official Companion*, London: Weidenfeld & Nicolson.

Smith, Julia and Holland, Tony (1987) *EastEnders: The Inside Story*, London: BBC Books.

Figure 9.6 References

The index

The index of a book is often the most helpful guide to the detail of its contents. A quick scan through the index will show you whether the kinds of topics in which you are interested feature in the book. Look out especially for topics of interest to you that have many page references.

Previewing a book can show you which parts of it may be most useful for your research and how thoroughly you need to read particular sections. It may be that only a small part of the book will be useful; it is unlikely that you will need to read the whole book.

► A book that seems too difficult to understand at the start of your research may be easier to understand later. If a book seems too difficult, take a note of its title and location in the library, in case you want to come back to it.

 Previewing a book for your project

Select from the library a book that relates to your research project (see Chapter 8 for how to use libraries).

Preview the book using the questions outlined in the section headed 'The components of a book' (pp. 118–20) and write a brief evaluation of its relevance to your investigation.

PRIMARY AND SECONDARY SOURCES

► **Primary sources**: the first account of the data, or the data itself.

► **Secondary sources**: reviews of or commentaries on primary sources.

When you are choosing written material to help you in your project you need to know whether the source is primary or secondary. This will help you to identify the author's purposes and any underlying assumptions. **Primary sources** are first-hand accounts not based on other written works, nor reinterpreted by other researchers. In documentary research, primary sources are original documents such as diaries, company reports, official documents, a company's equal opportunity policy statement, or a record of transactions completed. In scientific research, a primary source is usually something within an experiment such as change in the behaviour of a cell culture. In social research, primary sources can be people who are directly observed, or the answers they give to questions.

Secondary sources, on the other hand, draw upon and discuss primary sources and therefore come into being later than the primary source. Secondary sources are generally in the form of commentaries, reviews, opinions, critiques, interpretations and other researchers' findings.

 Primary or secondary?

Listed below are descriptions or titles of some primary and secondary sources for the history of sixteenth-century Europe. Decide which are primary and which are secondary sources. If in doubt, check with your tutor.

> Knox, John. *The History of the Reformation in Scotland* (first published 1587).
> Koenigsberger, H.G. and Mosse, George L. *Europe in the Sixteenth Century* (first published 1968).
> Reports of the Venetian Ambassadors to the Venetian Senate, covering the years 1496–1533.
> Machiavelli, N. *The Prince* (completed in 1516, first published 1530).
> Clark, Sir George. *Early Modern Europe* (editions 1954, 1957, 1960).
> Journals of the House of Lords (1510–1614).

Both primary and secondary sources are important when undertaking research. It is not necessarily the case that primary sources are superior to secondary sources; all sources of data have strengths and weaknesses. However, if your instructions require you to study primary data rather than relying on secondary sources, you must do so.

► See 'Bias' later in this chapter (p. 130).

> When previewing books or any other publications, remember to keep asking yourself whether the contents are relevant to your research topic.

APPROACHES TO READING

Once you have selected a book or article you need to decide how to read it. The approach you adopt depends on the nature of the reading material and what you want to get out of it.

Are you going to read the book:

- to provide background for your research task?
- to gain an overall impression of the book and its central ideas or facts?
- to find a specific piece of information?
- to understand the whole book in detail?

Reading for background

When you read to gather general background on your research sub-

▶ Examples of the use of background reading as part of formal research are:

- reading a historical novel before researching the historical period in which the novel is set;
- reading the biography of a successful business figure before making a detailed study of his or her company.

ject you probably read fairly quickly, skimming or browsing through the text, pausing from time to time when a particular paragraph attracts your attention. This type of reading can be an enjoyable way of getting yourself into the right frame of mind for studying your research topic more systematically. It can be done outside 'study times' and does not necessarily entail taking notes or remembering what you read in any detail.

Reading for an overview

If you need to obtain an overview of the book and identify its central themes, ideas or facts, you must take a more disciplined approach than you would for background reading. You are reading:

- to find out how the book might be useful for your research project;
- to decide whether you want to read all or part of the book in more detail.

> Reading to form an overall impression entails:
>
> - reading quite rapidly;
> - reading the introductory and concluding paragraphs and noting the main themes or facts.

▶ To test whether you have picked up the central ideas or facts of a book or article, write them down briefly or explain them to someone else.

You are not concerned with details or with a complete understanding of the material. Once you have taken an overview you can read rather more slowly and in depth so that the structure of the book and its central ideas become clearer. Make use of chapter headings and subheadings, any summaries, recapitulations, section reviews, margin notes and so on. Look for key phrases in the first lines of paragraphs such as 'First of all', 'Finally', 'By contrast' or 'In summary'.

Reading for specific information

To find a specific piece of information use all available pointers such as the table of contents, index, chapter headings and subheadings to guide you to the item or section you want. Then scan the section to see if it is really relevant. If it is, read the section again slowly and thoroughly. You will probably want to make notes at this point.

Reading for critical understanding

This is the most thorough approach to reading and should be followed if your purpose is to understand material thoroughly so that you can build on it in further research. You should be able to:

- identify the assumptions underlying the text and evaluate its usefulness to your research;

- follow a complex argument;
- understand each stage of an experiment, observation or survey in order to repeat it yourself.

First, read for an overview and to identify the central ideas or facts. Then read through the material more slowly in detail, taking note of the structure and underlying assumptions and evaluating the arguments. This does not necessarily entail reading every page word by word but you must read actively, understanding each section as you go, so that when you have finished reading you can reproduce clearly what you have read. Take notes or underline (only if the book belongs to you) to help your understanding. As you read, look for information to help you identify the author's purpose and assumptions and to understand the content. The box below suggests some of the questions you might ask yourself as you read. This will help to give you a detailed critical understanding of a piece of written material.

Questions to ask as you read for understanding

What is the author's purpose? Is this stated explicitly or is there a hidden agenda?

Who is the intended audience?

What are the author's assumptions and are they explicitly stated?

Which aspects of the subject area has the author chosen to focus on and which to omit?

Is the content presented in breadth or in depth?

What is the main argument, theme or concept and how is it developed?

What evidence or explanation is used to support the main points?

Is the author's purpose influenced by a contemporary issue or by a particular approach or value judgement?

Is the author defending a particular point of view?

Is there any evidence of deliberate bias or discrimination in language or attitudes?

Do the facts seem correct?

Does the content answer any of your questions about the subject?

How are the contents related to what you know about the subject?

Does the conclusion relate to the introduction and the rest of the contents?

Is any material included that is irrelevant to your research topic?

If you find it difficult to answer the questions in the box above, find someone else to discuss the material with. Ask the person to read the section that you are having trouble with and discuss any differences of opinion. A fresh eye can often help to clarify difficult material and enhance your own understanding. While you are reading and evaluating how useful a particular piece of material will be, you should also be thinking about which information you want to make notes of and how you are going to record and file these notes.

BIAS

One of the areas you must consider as you read is that of bias. Texts, whether primary or secondary sources, are produced for different purposes, and some may have the effect of introducing bias. It is important for the researcher to be aware of and identify bias so that findings are not distorted.

The first step in identifying bias is to decide whether the source is primary or secondary (see pp. 126–7). Next, think about the purposes the author had for producing the text. It is tempting to believe, for example, that an official government report on education is a reliable and relatively unbiased source.

Official government texts are a rich and useful source for the researcher, often representing an extensive range of oral and documentary evidence researched by experts in the field. However, those same experts invited to report on a particular aspect of education are often chosen because their views accord with those of the government, and they are 'respectable' members of society. This means that there may be both a political and a social-class bias in the views expressed and that more radical and critical views have been left out. It may be that any evidence that did not conform to the 'official' view was omitted.

Even a diary, which one might expect to be particularly frank and honest, must be considered for bias. For whose eyes was the diary written? It is human nature to select and present facts in such a way as to put the writer in the most favourable light should the diary be read in the future. Remember that any personal texts, such as letters, diaries, autobiographies and life stories, inevitably contain a measure of bias because they are subjective accounts of events.

The use of newspapers as a source can be problematic unless the researcher is on the look-out for evidence of bias. The most obvious bias operating in newspapers is political, with the majority of our national daily press being identified with right-wing opinion. The reader also has to contend with the way in which certain items are reported. What is regarded as newsworthy by the popular press may not be given coverage by the quality press and vice versa. This emphasis could distort the findings of a researcher who was using newspapers as a source for interpreting, for example, the conduct of a war.

Looking at newspapers

Go to your local library and look at accounts of a major news event as it appears in a tabloid newspaper (such as *The Sun*, the *Daily Mirror* or the *News of the World*) and then in a quality newspaper (such as the *Guardian*, *The Times*, the *Daily Telegraph*, *The Independent* or the *Financial Times*). Read both accounts carefully and answer the following questions:

(a) How do the two stories differ in the headlines, content and pictures used?
(b) How does the style of writing and language used differ?
(c) Can you identify any bias in the reporting?

You will get more out of this exercise if someone else does it too and you can discuss your findings together. To add an extra dimension to this exercise, compare a television channel's treatment of the same news story.

NOTE-MAKING

The amount of note-making you do and the form it takes can vary. Some research topics involve more note-making than others. You should usually aim to keep your notes as brief as possible without losing the essence of what you want to record. Ending up with pages of detailed notes may give you the feeling you have done a lot of work, but these notes are of little value if you have no idea how to organize or use them. If you have defined your research topic carefully before reading, you should be able to take fewer notes. To some extent the amount of detail you record depends on whether you can easily get access to the material again.

If you judge that you will need the material later, at the very least you need to record a bare outline of its contents and where to find it again.

How to make notes

Notes are best kept in a loose-leaf file. This gives you the flexibility to arrange and rearrange them as your knowledge and understanding increase. You can file your notes together by topic rather than in the order in which they happen to be written. Where material is relevant to more than one topic, you can make cross-references between one section and another. It is a good idea to develop your own method of note-making and to remain as consistent as possible so that you appreciate the significance of the notes you have made several weeks and many books later. Below are some suggestions for good practice.

> **Good practice in note-making**
> • Use headings to help you group facts or ideas in a way that is meaningful to you.

▶ Making notes doesn't mean copying bits out of books.

▶ Note-making:
• keeps you active when studying – you concentrate better and retain more;
• helps you to develop your powers of selection, analysis and criticism;
• provides a written, organized record for your research report.

- Use section numbering (this can be based on numbers, letters or a mixture of the two).
- Use capitals to make significant words stand out.
- Use underlining to give emphasis or draw attention.
- Use coloured pens or highlighters (but always use them consistently).
- Use abbreviations (see the list below).
- Use file-spacers to keep different kinds of notes separate in your file.
- *Always* record the source of your notes.

It is also vitally important that you accurately record all your sources, so that you can refer to or quote from them later (see Chapter 11: 'Writing up'). You may find that underlining or highlighting text is useful, but you should do this only if the written material belongs to you. If you find a piece of writing that is particularly significant you may wish to photocopy it for future reference. You can then use underlining as your method of noting relevant passages or phrases. However, it is a good idea to try to express in your own words and as succinctly as possible the gist of what you have read and to keep notes separately from their source. After all, you have done the hard slog of reading through the material and you will probably not have enough time to read through it all again when you are under the pressure of meeting deadlines.

Quoting and referencing

Whenever you consult a piece of published writing, write down full details of the author, title and publication date. Then on each page of notes relating to that work write the title or author and list the book's or article's page numbers in the margin of your notes. You should get into this habit from the very beginning of your research project because it is essential for quoting and referencing. Use quotation marks to indicate clearly the beginning and end of material that you have copied word for word.

Useful abbreviations

e.g.	for example (Latin: *exempli gratia*)
i.e.	that is (Latin: *id est*)
cf.	compare (Latin: *confer*), remember in this context
NB	note well (Latin: *nota bene*), important
=	equals, is the same as
<	less than, fewer than
>	greater than, more than
∴	therefore
∵	because
ibid.	in the same place (Latin: *ibidem*), i.e. the quotation comes from the book last given as a reference
c.	about (Latin: *circa*), approximately
et al.	and others (Latin: *et alii*), usually refers to authors
MS	manuscript (Latin: *manuscriptum*)

MSS	manuscripts
passim	(Latin) here and there, throughout; usually refers to something occurring in various places in the text
p.	page
pp.	pages
ff.	and following, e.g. p. 26 ff.
op. cit.	in the work quoted (Latin: *opere citato*), referring to a work that has already been referred to
[*sic*]	thus, so; used when an apparent error is an accurate copy of the source
viz.	namely (Latin: *videlicet*)

If you use these abbreviations in your final report, you will need to punctuate them correctly. Most dictionaries have a listing of abbreviations with correct punctuation. In your notes, you needn't bother about this.

What to note

What you note depends on the focus of your research topic, but the box outlines some of the most likely areas that you will need to record.

What to note

Your notes should include:

- the source of the notes you are taking;
- central ideas, themes or facts that are relevant to your research;
- the authors' purposes, assumptions and biases;
- quotations that are pertinent to your topic and/or sum up what the author is saying;
- useful statistics or other details;
- items to follow up, for instance:
  - questions prompted by the text
  - a line of enquiry to pursue
  - an opinion you disagree with
  - references to other works you need to look at.

How to keep records

Finding information in the first place can often be quite difficult. Finding the same piece of information again, often some time afterwards, can be even harder unless your methods of making and filing notes are thorough and systematic. Some researchers recommend that you keep a special research notebook, in which you record all activities relating to your research project – the dates questionnaires were sent out and returned; dates of visits to libraries, museums, etc.; good ideas and questions and so on.

► **Research diaries** record what you did in your project and when you did it. They are sometimes required for assessment of your project and in some kinds of courses, including GNVQ, they could be useful evidence of your Information Retrieval and Time Management skills which will count towards your final grade.

► Card indexes are very useful for storing references.

► If you make references in your notes, always make them in full, using the style you will be required to quote them in. This can save hours and hours of work when you write up your project.

► A **computer database** operates on similar principles to a card index system but is much more powerful and flexible. If you have access to database software it is worthwhile considering creating your own database to store and retrieve information. It will also enable you to display evidence of Information Technology skills.

Such a notebook gives a useful chronological record of the progress of your project. If you use a loose-leaf binder for this purpose, you can maintain a flexible record that can be added to in a logical and accessible way. Keeping loose-leaf notes helps you to sort and file your information in a variety of ways. You may wish to file your notes under different subject headings, by stages of your research, by names of authors you have consulted or by more than one of these methods, and use a system of cross-referencing.

Card indexes

One of the most reliable and flexible methods of keeping records of publications you have consulted is the card index. If you are undertaking a research project of any size this will save you time and considerable frustration in the long run. In the early days of an investigation it may seem adequate to jot down a reference or a note on a scrap of paper, but as your research proceeds you will find you have accumulated many pieces of information and that your references are incomplete, muddled or misplaced. The advantage of recording information on cards is that you can insert later entries and re-sort the cards if necessary.

Index cards can be obtained from stationers. They come in different sizes: 5 × 3 inches, 6 × 4 inches or 8 × 5 inches. The larger the card you use, the more information you can record. You should give each card a short title. When you have made your notes on the cards, file them in alphabetical order of title. You can add more information to the cards either by writing on the back of them or stapling additional material to them.

The cards should provide complete references and include all the information you are likely to need to locate the source again (including the need for interlibrary loan applications) and for compiling the references or bibliography for your project report. Cards may also include notes about the content of the book or article, reminders about where to locate useful information in the text, useful quotations and so on (see 'What to note', p. 133). You should always make a note of all the books, articles or reports you have consulted. In the case of a text that you did not find particularly useful to your project, you should note down the reasons why. This may save you time in the future when you come across the reference and may be tempted to borrow the book again, forgetting that you had already decided the work was of no interest to your line of enquiry.

It is a good idea to keep simple model cards that remind you about which details should be noted, together with the punctuation and layout of an accepted reference system (see 'Bibliographies and references', Chapter 11, pp. 164–5). Whichever reference system you use you will always need the following information:

Books

- author's surname and forename or initials;
- date of publication;

Elliot, J. (1991),

Action Research for Educational Change,
London, Open University Press

Bracht, G.H. and Glass, G.V. (1968),

'The external validity of experiments',
American Educational Research Journal,
Vol. 5, Autumn, pp. 437–74

Hounsell, D. (1984),

'Learning and essay writing',
in F. Marton et al. (1984),
The Experience of Learning,
Edinburgh, Scottish Academic Press,
pp. 103–23

Figure 9.7 Index cards for sources. These cards use the Harvard system of referencing: (a) books; (b) articles in journals; (c) articles in collections

- title (underlined);
- place of publication;
- name of publisher.

Articles
- author's surname and forename or initials;
- date of publication;
- title (in quotation marks);
- source of the article, namely:
     In journals:
     - title of journal (underlined);
     - volume number;
     - date of issue;

        • page numbers;

or

   In collections:
- author/editor;
- date;
- title of book (underlined);
- place of publication;
- name of publisher;
- page numbers.

You should develop a modified version of these headings for company reports and other official publications.

It is also useful to note any information that will help you to locate the book or article again. For example, you might wish to record that you originally found the book in a particular library or that a friend has a copy. If you have borrowed the book from a local library you may wish to note the Dewey Decimal number.

The ISBN number (International Standard Book Number), which is a number unique to the publication concerned, is extremely useful if you are requesting a book on interlibrary loan, or if you want to buy your own copy.

Noting quotations

A quotation can often illustrate a point you wish to make in your report or add an extra dimension to your argument. It is important to make a full and accurate copy of the quotation at the time you read it, because you will not have time to recall books from the library or search for scraps of paper when you are writing up your final report.

► See Chapter 11 for more information on using quotations in writing up reports.

If a particular sentence or paragraph appears to be potential quotation material, copy it carefully and record the details of the author and publication together with the chapter and page number. The quoted material should be presented within quotation marks and if you have left out any words this should be made clear to the reader.

CHAPTER SUMMARY

This chapter was designed to help you to:

- scan books and other written materials to see if they are relevant for your needs – this is often called 'doing a literature search';
- read materials in different ways for different purposes;
- look out for bias in the materials you read;
- make notes that will be genuinely useful to you in conducting your project and writing it up.

There is more material on reading and writing in Chapter 11.

Organizing your data

WHY IS GOOD ORGANIZATION IMPORTANT?

If you have followed the advice given in the previous chapters, you will have designed your project to make sure you can collect the best possible data within the time, the resources and the size of sample available to you.

All the time you have been carrying out your research, you have been making decisions about which questions to ask, what to observe, what data to collect, which experiments to do and how to do them. All these decisions are aspects of being organized in your research, and decisions about what you do with your data form part of this process.

Starting with the first piece of data that you collect, you must record and organize it into some kind of system that enables you to retrieve it when you need it. This is especially true if you are doing exploratory research and you start the project without knowing where it is going to end up.

You will create major problems for yourself if you wait until all your data is collected before you get it into shape. For example:

- You will eventually sit down in front of a pile of paper, pages of figures or stacks of tapes and have no idea where to start.
- You may find that you have wasted a lot of time collecting data that is not relevant to the question you are investigating.
- You may find that important pieces of data are missing and it is too late to do anything about it.

▶ Sampling was discussed in Chapter 6, pp. 80–92.

▶ If you are doing a GNVQ course, make sure that you are familiar with the 'grading criteria', especially those concerned with information seeking and handling.

- You are unlikely to get the best from the data you have because you will have to work on it in a hurry in order to meet the deadline for handing in your report.

▶ Be aware of word limits.

There is another reason for keeping track of your data as you collect it, and this is related to word limits. You will usually have been given an approximate word limit for your report, so you will have a rough idea of how much you can write. This, in turn, gives you some idea of how much data you will need and how detailed it should be. If you do not take this limit into account, you will finish up with a mass of data that, however good it may be, you will not be able to use in your report. You should, however, check with your tutor on whether you are allowed to include raw or unprocessed data in an appendix without this counting against your word limit.

▶ See Chapter 11, pp. 159–62, for guidance on the structure of final reports.

Working to a word limit

Let's suppose that you have been told that your project should result in a report of around 2,000 words. Your tutor may give you further advice on this, but the word limit does not usually include diagrams, references or appendices.

Once you know your word limit, make a list of what you think the sections or chapters might be and estimate how many words you should allocate to each. This can guide you as you collect the data and as you write the report. For example, if you have 2,000 words in total and you think you can spare 250 for the introduction, then you can be sure that if you have written an introduction of 1,000 words you are on the wrong track. Here is an example of a student's initial plan for a project report of 2,000 words:

Introduction and aim of project	250 words
Review of previous research on this topic	300 words
Description of research methods	250 words
Results	450 words
Discussion of results	450 words
Conclusion and recommendations	300 words
Total	2,000 words

You can see that with 2,000 words there is not much room for manoeuvre.

WHAT SORT OF DATA ARE YOU COLLECTING?

▶ Are you using quantitative or qualitative data?

How you organize your data depends a lot on what sort of data you are collecting. A distinction has already been made (Chapter 4, pp. 50–2) between research that results in data in the form of numbers, or quantitative data, and research that results in data without numbers (mostly words or illustrations), or qualitative data. Some data is a mixture of the two.

Quantitative data

You might collect the following types of quantitative data:

- the numerical and statistical results of experiments;
- various kinds of counts, such as the numerical results of questionnaires, the number of customers in a shopping mall or the number of units produced in a factory;
- data where you have put things in some sort of rank order, perhaps of importance, or of quality, or of value;
- data where you have asked people to express an opinion or an attitude by choosing from a fixed range of answers;
- financial data;
- demographic data.

Qualitative data

You might collect the following types of qualitative data:

- the descriptive results of experiments;
- quotations from questionnaires or interviews where you have invited people to give a free or open response, perhaps for a piece of market research or opinion polling;
- notes of your observations of people's actions – you may have observed them directly or you may have recorded them on audio or video tape;
- various types of documents you have collected such as maps, photographs, letters, minutes of meetings, promotional materials or company reports.

Organizing quantitative data

There is something neat about figures and statistics. People tend to respect and believe things that are stated in numbers. Numbers can be very persuasive, so you should be very careful about how you collect, record and display quantitative data.

First, it is important to record any figures neatly in a suitable place, which is likely to be a notebook rather than separate pieces of paper. Remember that it can be easy to confuse some handwritten figures, such as '1' and '7'.

It is easy to lose decimal points or to 'find' or 'lose' zeros in large numbers, thereby changing the result by factors of ten, which will be thoroughly misleading.

Always include full details of any numbers. This should include the units of measurement where necessary, the date when the data was collected and any other details that will enable you to understand and evaluate the figures later on. This may seem to be stating the obvious, but it is surprising how quickly notes become meaningless if their context is not clear.

When taking measurements, never pretend that you can measure more accurately than the limits of your equipment or scales. This is especially true when you do further work on the figures using a calculator. For example, if you measure weights to two

▶ Putting a dash across the figure 7 can avoid confusing it with the figure 1.
▶ When producing columns of figures, it is best to align the decimal points one above another.

▶ If you are recording your data using a computer, these points are just as important. Also, do not forget to copy your data onto back-up disks in case you lose your originals.

decimal places then it would not be appropriate to give a final result to five decimal places.

Common sense, and the ability to make reasonable estimates, should set alarm bells ringing if you have made serious mistakes in your readings, recordings or calculations.

 Without doing any serious calculating, can you spot why this average must be wrong?

Ages of children in sample (years): 2, 2, 2, 3, 4, 5, 5, 5, 6, 7, 8, 9, 9, 9
Average age: 8 years

And can you see why these percentages must be wrong?

Percentage of respondents choosing each option:
A: 11   B: 15   C: 24   D: 27   E: 14   F: 31   G: 9
    H: 17

If you are using a database on a computer, you may be able to set it to reject any data that is obviously wrong. For example, if you are inputting prices (in pence) of 500 gm chocolate bars, then you could set it to reject any input over 1,000.

Always be honest about the results you get, providing you have checked the figures and are confident that they are right. You will learn a lot more from trying to explain an unexpected result than from attempting to 'massage' the figures to give the result you think they should.

Don't forget the importance, particularly in science, of taking extra or 'replicate' measurements to check earlier ones. Never rely on just one count or reading. In many scientific experiments you are likely to take a number of readings and then to take an average of those readings. The same would probably be true if you were counting passengers on a daily train service or the numbers using a Tourist Information office. In some cases, such as analysis by titration in chemistry, you would also expect individual readings in the group not to differ from one another by more than a certain amount.

Presenting quantitative data

When presenting quantitative data, you will want it to be neat, clear and laid out in an attractive, eye-catching and informative way. It is an old cliché, but a picture can be worth a thousand words by making information much easier to understand. Consider the following example:

In a particular school in 1991, a researcher noted that five out of the forty-five (11 per cent) of those who took A level Geography obtained an A grade whereas fifteen (33 per cent) obtained a B grade and fifteen (33 per cent) a C grade. In the following year, when there were

▶ **Bar charts, pie charts, histograms, pictograms, graphs** and **tables** are all ways of presenting quantitative data pictorially. Publications such as *Social Trends* provide excellent examples and will give you ideas for your own work.

forty students, 5 per cent obtained an A grade, 20 per cent a B grade and 15 per cent a C grade.

Even in this simple example, it is much easier to compare the results in 1993 and 1994 when they are presented as a bar chart (see Figure 10.1).

► Note how the chart has been clearly labelled.

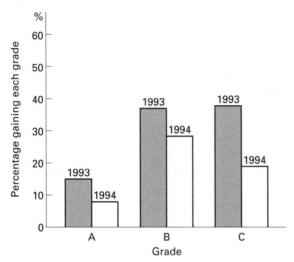

Figure 10.1 Bar chart showing A-level geography grades over two years

Bar charts

As shown in the example above, a bar chart displays quantitative data in 'bars' set against two axes. One axis shows the headings or categories for the data; the other shows the scale against which the quantity in each bar is drawn. Bars can be drawn vertically or horizontally, there is no limit on the number of bars that can be included, and the width of each bar should be the same. Bars should not touch each other, except where a comparison is being made within a category (see Figure 10.1).

Pie charts

In pie charts, proportions, or shares of a total, are represented by angles within the 'pie' and the size of the 'slices'. Figure 10.2 shows an example of a pie chart used in a project that investigated the running of a catering business, to show the types of functions catered for from May to September in a particular year.

► In a pie chart, the total of 100 per cent should be thought of as made up of 360 degrees or 60 minutes on a clock-face. When drawing precise pie charts, use a protractor.

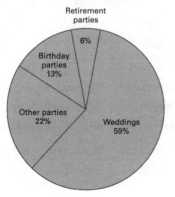

Figure 10.2 Pie chart showing types of functions catered for from May to September 1994

Histograms

It is easy to confuse bar charts with histograms, but there is an important difference between them. In a bar chart, the height (or length) of the bar reflects the quantity to be displayed. The width of the bar is simply the choice of the person designing the bar chart.

Histograms are used when data is grouped into ranges, and the width of the bar in a histogram reflects the size of the range. This is much easier to explain through an example. Imagine that you are researching the relationship between people's ages and their choice of holiday destination. You have arranged with a local travel agent that it will supply you with raw data about bookings it has received (though it will not, of course, give you any individual names). You receive data about 174 people, with ages ranging from 20 to 69 years, who have booked holidays to three different destinations. You do not want to present each individual case, but rather to present the data in age-groups. You therefore group the individuals accordingly and produce histograms of the type shown in Figure 10.3. Note that the bars are in contact with each other; this is not necessary in a bar chart.

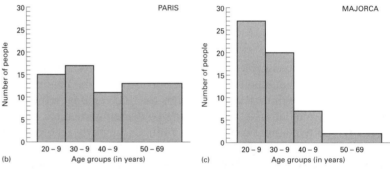

Figure 10.3 Histograms showing the relation between people's age and their choice of holiday destination

Pictograms

In a pictogram, quantities are represented by small drawings. For example, Figure 10.4 shows a pictogram for a project that included a traffic survey, showing the numbers of cars passing a particular place at various times.

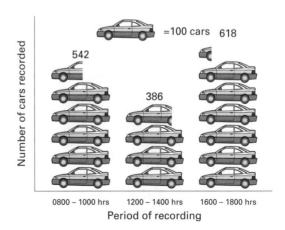

Figure 10.4 Pictogram depicting numbers of cars passing a particular place at various times of day

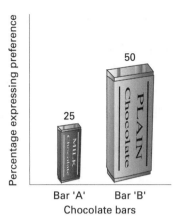

Figure 10.5 A misleading pictogram

Pictograms become misleading if differences in the quantities recorded are displayed disproportionately. This usually happens when a three-dimensional symbol is used. Thus the pictogram in Figure 10.5 does not correctly represent the relation between bar A and bar B, since in bar B both the height (length) and the width have been doubled. Bar B should have twice the area of bar A, but the way it has been drawn gives it four times the area.

Graphs

Bar charts, pie charts and histograms can be very effective ways of displaying quantities at a given time. Sometimes, however, you will want to show how two measurements vary in relation to each

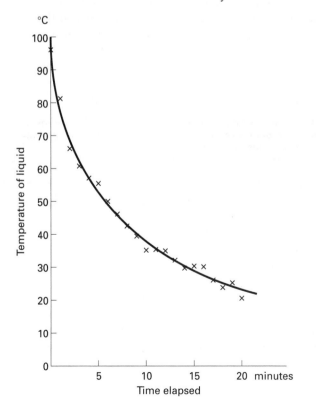

Figure 10.6 Graph showing heat loss over time

other, such as the falling temperature of a liquid over time after a heat source has been turned off (as shown in Figure 10.6). In other contexts, you may want to show changes in the unit costs of production in relation to the number of items produced, or how prices change in relation to demand. The best way to display such relationships is to draw a graph. As in all diagrams, remember to label the graph fully, so that the reader can easily understand what is being shown.

When you plot the points on a graph, it is unlikely that they will make a perfect curve. In this case, the curve you draw should be the one that best fits the data, as illustrated in Figure 10.6.

Tables

Where figures cannot be represented in any of the graphic forms that have been shown above, it may be best to set them out in the form of a table. For instance, a chemistry student might do an experiment to measure the alkalinity of a solution. To do this, the student would first measure out a set quantity of the solution, usually 25 ml, into a beaker, and then add a couple of drops of indicator. Using a piece of equipment called a burette, which is a calibrated tube with a stopcock at one end, an acid solution (of a known concentration) would be added drop by drop until the solution in the beaker changed colour. (The colour change is caused by the indicator and occurs when the solution becomes neutral.) The student would take two readings from the burette: the initial volume of acid solution, and the amount left in the burette when the solution changed colour. The difference between these two readings would then be used to calculate the concentration of the alkaline solution. This process is known as 'titration'. The researcher would normally take one set of trial readings, followed by three sets of readings on which to base the conclusion. The readings would be tabulated as shown in Table 10.1.

► Many word-processing or graphics packages will generate bar charts, pie charts, histograms or graphs. Use this facility if you have access to it.

Table 10.1 Tables like this one can be used to present the results of experiments requiring certain measurements – in this case titration – to be carried out a number of times

	Trial	1	2	3
Second Reading	21.8 ml	22.54 ml	21.42 ml	22.63 ml
First Reading	0.5 ml	1.26 ml	0.16 ml	1.35 ml
Acid solution titrated	21.3 ml	21.28 ml	21.26 ml	21.28 ml

The best estimate is considered to be the average of the three readings, that is: 21.27 ml.

As a further example, suppose a researcher wants to assess the effectiveness of an exercise programme. First, she tests a group of athletes to measure their fitness (we shall not concern ourselves here with how this is done). After they have followed a programme of exercises over a number of weeks, she gives them the same test again. The results could be given as shown in Table 10.2.

► Remember that the average must also be expressed to two decimal places. The readings are likely to vary because of random errors introduced throughout, inaccurate measurement of the first 25 ml, inconsistency in deciding the exact point at which the solution changes colour, or even temperature fluctuations during the experiment.

Table 10.2 Tables like this one giving athletes' fitness scores can be a clear way of presenting 'before and after' data for ease of comparison

Person	Before	After	Change
1	45	55	+10
2	42	48	+6
3	36	36	0
4	59	63	+4
5	48	53	+5
6	45	48	+3

MAKING SENSE OF QUANTITATIVE DATA

Having presented your quantitative data in one or more of the ways described above, you have to explain what can be learned from the data. What conclusions can you draw from the results? How do they compare with other similar studies? Can you explain how and why you arrived at your conclusion? Remember that there is no such thing as a 'good' result in this context; providing you have designed your research well and carried it out carefully, then the result is as it is. The important thing is that you have demonstrated your research skills and that you can give a reasonable explanation of why the results have come out as they have.

Making comparisons

Drawing conclusions and identifying causes almost always involve making comparisons between data and situations. For example, if you have produced data in the form of bar charts or pie charts, what can you say about the sizes of the bars or the 'slices' of the pie, in relation to each other? What comparisons can you make? Can you draw any conclusions from these? You can ask similar questions about pictograms, graphs and histograms.

For example, if you look again at Figure 10.1, what can you say about the two sets of examination results? Clearly the results in 1992 were not as good as those in 1991. Why might this be? Incidentally, you should be cautious about making comparisons like this with only two years' results. You really need more years to get an idea of a general direction or trend. Perhaps 1991 was an abnormally good year in a run of years like 1992, or vice versa.

When making comparisons between quantitative data, it is usually better to express the quantities in percentages rather than as simple numbers. In Figure 10.1, this gave us a more convenient way of comparing the two years than if we had known only that five out of forty-five gained an A grade in 1991 whereas two out of forty did in 1992. It is the proportion gaining each grade that was important rather than the number, and percentages are a very useful way of expressing proportions. Five A grades from five students (100 per cent) might be considered better than ten A grades from 100 students (10 per cent).

In some cases, especially when making comparisons, it is valuable to calculate the average of sets of figures. For example, average life expectancy is often used as an indicator to compare the standard of living in different countries, or in different regions of the same country. Average weekly patient 'throughput' over a period of time may be used to compare the efficiency of two hospitals.

> **Calculating average values**
>
> The most familiar sort of 'average' used in everyday life is more precisely termed the '**mean**'. This is the figure you get by adding all the scores and dividing by the number of scores. Statisticians also use:
>
> **mode:** the most frequently occurring score
> **median:** the middle score in a series

► There are other useful statistical measures, such as the 'standard deviation', but these are outside the scope of this book.

It may also be useful to calculate the **range**; this is the difference between the highest and lowest figures in the data collected.

Statistical testing

Statisticians might want to ask more searching questions such as:

- Is there more variation *within* each group that I am investigating than *between* those groups?

► This sort of question is important when you are testing hypotheses.

There may not be much value in making comparisons between groups if the variations within each group are too great. We may discover, for example, that one group has a higher average IQ than another, but this tells us nothing about the range of IQs within either group. One group might contain a few very high and a few very low scorers, while members of the other group might score about the same.

- How confident am I that the result that I got from my research happened because of my experimental approach rather than simply by chance?

Statistical tests are used to answer specialized questions such as these. Remember, if you intend to test your data statistically, then you must take advice from a statistician *before* you start collecting it. This is because data that is to be subjected to statistical tests usually has to be collected and organized in particular ways.

Correlations and causes

► Two variables **correlate** when they vary in relation to each other. When they move in the same direction they are **positively** correlated. When they move in opposite directions they are **negatively** correlated.

When two sets of figures appear to vary in relation to each other, you must be very careful before deciding that one thing is the cause of the other. For example, you may ask a group of students to state how many hours of each day they spend studying, and you might then compare this to their scores in an examination. You may find that the two are related – that those with more hours of study tend to get higher marks. But can you say that longer study time is a *cause* of higher marks? Not necessarily, there might be other explanations. One of these is the exact opposite: that those who have consistently achieved higher scores in the past are motivated to study more. There might be a completely separate factor that affects *both* variables, such as keeping fit. Perhaps people who take more exercise (a) have more stamina for study and (b) do better in examinations. Figure 10.7 depicts some of the possible relationships.

▶ It is always worth playing with diagrams like the one shown in Figure 10.7 to identify all the possible ways in which two variables might be related.

▶ The fact that two variables correlate does not necessarily mean that one causes the other.

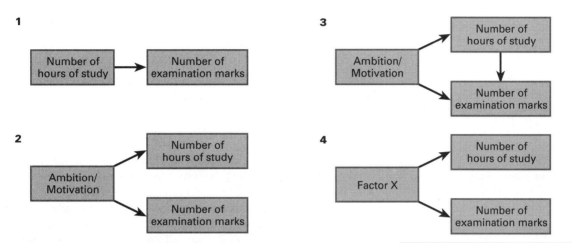

Figure 10.7 Possible explanations for the correlation between number of hours of study and exam results

ORGANIZING QUALITATIVE DATA

The most straightforward qualitative data consists of descriptions of what took place, expressed in words. These descriptions (or 'accounts') should be as accurate and detailed as possible. In many cases, especially with scientific experiments, you can use diagrams to help improve and clarify a description. You may remember that a series of diagrams was planned to illustrate the outcome of the 'Maltese Cross' experiment in Chapter 4. In addition to diagrams, you can also use tables to describe what happened during an experiment or some other sort of trial exercise. The framework shown in Table 10.3 is an example.

Table 10.3 This table has been used to demonstrate the correlation observed between two variables: prices and sales

Price-cut c. 16%

| Item | Before | | After | |
	Price	Sales	Price	Sales
1	£1.50	150	£1.25	160
2	£3.00	160	£2.50	200
3	£4.50	160	£3.75	240

Conclusion: the same percentage price cut produces a greater increase in unit sales in higher-priced products.

Using the figures in Table 10.3, how would you decide whether the price cuts had resulted in higher sales revenue? And what information would you need in order to decide which prices result in the highest overall profit?

Other types of qualitative data include your own notes, audio tapes, answers to open questions in questionnaires and interviews, and anything else that comes in the form of words rather than numbers. Pictures and photographs may also be used as qualitative data.

How can you best organize this data? Your aim must be to turn the raw data into a structured and descriptive summary. In doing this, you must also provide readers with enough original evidence, in the form of examples from your data, to enable them to judge whether your summary is justified and reasonable.

Sorting qualitative data into themes

The first thing to do is to identify the key points and the key themes that run through the data. In some cases, these will be easy to identify because you will have collected data around the themes that you chose at the planning stage. In more open-ended research, these themes will emerge during the process of data-collection as your informants talk and respond to your questions. However, even if you did start out with key issues in mind, be prepared to reorganize them in the light of your responses, to add new themes or to search for key ideas within the categories you have set.

▶ Start analysing and organizing data from day one.

The absolutely vital point to stress is that your search for key points and themes in your qualitative data must start from day one of the research, that is, with the very first responses that you collect. The longer you leave this task and the more data you collect, the harder it is to get started. If you leave it until you have received all your data, you will have to spend many hours reading and rereading a mass of data before you can identify any patterns.

How do you start? First, by reading, listening to or watching your first sets of data several times. What strikes you about the data? Do people seem to be saying the same sorts of things? Do they have the same concerns? Do they behave in similar ways?

Transcribing tapes

If you have recorded audio tapes, you will have to decide whether you are going to transcribe them on to paper. This can take a lot of time (certainly an hour or more for fifteen minutes of tape for a semi-skilled typist) and you should not do it unless you have to. If you do transcribe, do it very carefully. You may decide to transcribe just one tape or part of a tape to include in an appendix. You may be allowed (as in a GNVQ course) to include the original tape as part of your evidence.

Looking for themes in qualitative data – an example

Michael was doing participant observation research alongside his weekend job in a café. He didn't have any grand research idea to start with. He gave himself six weeks to find one, and after each day's work he wrote down as much as he could remember about what happened in a research diary. As he did this he began to notice that what staff said about customers when they were in the kitchen was very different from what staff said to and about customers in the public area of the café.

He began to focus his observations on the contrasts between 'front stage' and 'backstage' talk and behaviour. This focus allowed him to concentrate on fewer types of activity, and to collect more data about each type. He became more selective. As time went on he focused down even more and paid particular attention to those times when staff were at the counter, or at the kitchen door, in sight of both the customers and the backstage staff. He noticed the various ways in which staff were able to pass on an order to the kitchen, and to make fun of or make complaints about customers at the same time, without the customers realizing this.

The title he finally produced was:

> Managing the boundary: an observation of staff–customer relations in a café.

The data he used in his report was a set of very precise verbal descriptions of this 'boundary' behaviour in the café, supplemented with some other observations from a restaurant, and from a menswear shop.

► Homing in on key ideas is called **progressive focusing**.

A word of warning: if you are going to be editing, reducing or reordering your data, always keep one complete copy of the original safe and untampered with. Remember, this is your main or primary evidence and, if you cut it up, deface it or lose it, you will have big problems.

Once you have begun to identify some key points or ideas in your data, you should give each key idea a name. This might be one word or it might be a short phrase. For instance, a researcher investigating the feelings of parents with very young children interviewed a sample group and began to identify key ideas that kept recurring. She labelled these:

> 'Time for myself'   'Sleeping patterns'   'Pleasures'

before she started sorting out her data into these categories.

You are going to have quite a number of these themes and it is better if you have a label for them, even if you do not use that label in your final report. However, be careful that you continue to learn from your data. You may settle early on for a set of key ideas and then restrict yourself to collecting or picking out only evidence that

► When choosing your short words or phrases to label key points or ideas, use something you will easily remember.

▶ The problem of discarding evidence that doesn't fit your preconceived ideas is sometimes referred to as the **Procrustean Bed**. Procrustes was a character in Greek legend who cut bits off his victims to make them fit into a bed.

▶ In this case, the events described by the parents could equally well have been categorized under alternative themes such as 'communication' or 'milestones'. The same evidence can be used to illustrate more than one theme. This shows the sorts of problems faced by the researcher in deciding key points.

▶ **Coding data**: in research using structured questionnaires the coding happens *before* the quantitative data is collected. In less structured kinds of research, resulting in more qualitative data, you may code the data *after* it has been collected.

▶ Remember once again that you should use a copy and store your originals.

confirms those key ideas. This can seriously distort the research process. Even if you were open-minded when you started, you could very quickly become closed to new ideas. Keep reassessing your key points as you go along. Later in the research process, your key points may become more firmly established.

How many key ideas are you looking for? This depends on the size of your project. In some cases there may be only four or five key points. In a big project there could be many more. Don't start out looking for a particular number of points. As you work through the data, you will find that some of your categories overlap, or can be made into one larger group. Many may turn out not to be key points at all and you may eventually discard them.

Every time you read some of your data, or listen to a tape, and recognize something that relates to one of your key themes, this becomes part of your **evidence** for that key idea. For example, in the research on parents, the researcher identified a key theme that she labelled 'Pleasures'. She decided on this theme because parents talked about events such as watching the baby's eyes focusing on them during feeding, and the delight when the baby took its first step. What the parents actually said, the words they used, make up the researcher's evidence.

Organizing data around themes

Once you have read or heard various pieces of evidence in your data that have led you to identify certain key themes, and you have given those key themes labels, you will need some kind of system so that you can collect together all the evidence that relates to any one theme. Labelling your data according to whether it is evidence for a particular theme is called 'coding' the data. There are various ways to do this:

• Using a copy of the raw data, write the label for the theme next to each relevant piece of evidence. Alternatively, you can highlight relevant sections using highlighter pens of varying colours.
• Write the name of the theme on a large envelope, then take a copy of your notes, cut out the relevant pieces of evidence and put them in the envelope. If you cut up your copy like this, be absolutely sure to write the date and the name of the person concerned on each piece of paper. You will also need to be sure that you cut out the complete piece of evidence because you may want to quote it in your report.
• Using index cards, write the name of each theme at the top of a card and copy each relevant piece of evidence from your notes on to the card. Again, you will need to identify each piece of evidence with the date and name. Copying will have to be done very carefully. The items of evidence may be so long that, instead of copying them out, you write

on the card a reference to where the relevant evidence can be found among the original data.

- Create a file on your word-processor for each of the themes, and copy the relevant evidence into each file, rather as you did with the index cards.
- Set up a database on a computer, with files for each theme, and sort the raw data into the relevant file.

Focusing and checking

As you collect more data, you will be asking: 'Are the same points recurring?', 'Are there any surprises?' You will find it helpful to share your ideas with other students or with your tutor. If your tutor organizes group tutorials, make the most of them. Be willing to share your ideas and receive feedback, questions and criticisms. It can be quite a challenge to put yourself on the spot like this, but always think of how valuable it will be for your research. If you have a chance to present your research to a group, especially while it is still in progress, always leave enough time for – and positively encourage – questions or responses from group members.

> ### Developing and testing hypotheses
>
> It is possible to formulate and test hypotheses in this kind of qualitative research. For example, in the café customer-relations study mentioned earlier, Michael developed and tested the following hypothesis:
>
> > If managing the boundary is a learned skill, then new staff won't do it when they are first appointed, but will learn to do it thereafter.

Progressive focusing

As you work on more and more of your data and your key points are emerging and being strengthened, you may become aware of gaps in the data. Things may be talked about in later interviews that were not even mentioned in earlier ones. Is there any chance of going back to people you have already talked to? Do you need to modify your questions or observations on future occasions? You should think carefully about whether it would be right to make changes now. If you do note an important gap later on in your research, then all you may be able to do is to suggest in your final recommendations that this is a subject for future research.

Do you have the chance to check the ideas you are coming up with against what others have found in their research? Your early search for books and articles may have revealed whether other people have written or researched on the same or similar topics. You can compare their ideas with yours, but do this carefully and critically and beware of being swayed too much by what you read.

You just have to keep at it. Reread your data. Think about the

▶ Remember: *always* back up all your disks.

ideas that are evident in it. Gradually you will get down to those key points. You will then be able to organize your data into key themes and turn it into evidence that relates to your conclusions.

Identifying themes in advance

So far, we have concentrated on identifying themes and sorting and coding data during and after the data-collection process. In some kinds of research, observers spend the early stages of their project establishing the themes and codes, and then spend the majority of the research period putting these codes into effect. Alternatively, they may simply adopt a coding system already designed by someone else.

▶ See the observation schedule for observing nurses given in Chapter 5, p. 63.

For instance, researchers have produced various ways of coding the sorts of things that teachers do in classrooms. Teachers may 'give an instruction' or 'ask a question' or 'give praise'. In this kind of research, an observer would start with a list of codes and then, at set intervals, would code the teacher's behaviour against the correct code. The results of this will be quantitative data and can be summarized and presented using one of the methods we have already described.

▶ **Content analysis** produces quantitative data from qualitative sources. For example, the literary researcher may count the number of times a particular phrase is used by two different authors, or a media specialist might measure the space given to topics in a newspaper.

A similar procedure may be used when examining documents. In this case it is often referred to as 'content analysis' because you are looking at and analysing the contents of the documents (see pp. 64–5). For example, a researcher into children's literature might identify the number of times that boys are portrayed doing something exciting or heroic, compared with the number of times that girls are portrayed in the same way.

MAKING SENSE OF QUALITATIVE DATA

You may have already realized that organizing qualitative data, as described above, involves making sense of it at the same time. The main tasks when organizing your qualitative data were to identify the key points or themes arising from that data, to give them convenient labels, and to collect together the evidence relating to each. Making sense of your data is a matter of looking for patterns in the data that link your key points.

You may have had some previous experience of looking for patterns that link ideas. There are several simple techniques for doing this.

Spidergrams

Probably the most common technique is the 'spider' diagram. Here you start with a central idea and then radiate related ideas from it, and to each other, until you have what looks like a spider's web. Figure 10.8 is an example based on a project about why some people are more likely than others to claim welfare benefits.

Figure 10.8 A spidergram for thinking about why some people don't claim welfare benefits

Flow charts

If the key points fall logically into a sequence then a 'flow chart' would be a more appropriate diagram. Figure 10.9 shows a flow chart for the same project as the spidergram.

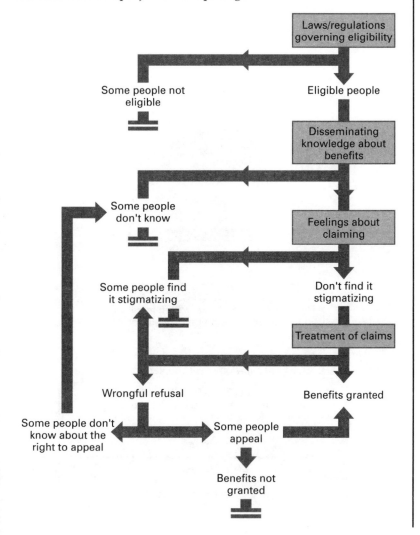

Figure 10.9 A flow chart for thinking about why some people don't claim welfare benefits

Other techniques

Other examples for linking ideas and themes are concentric circles and pyramids, maps and networks. Pyramids are often used when things are put in order of importance or seniority. Figures 10.10 to 10.14 are examples of these various techniques.

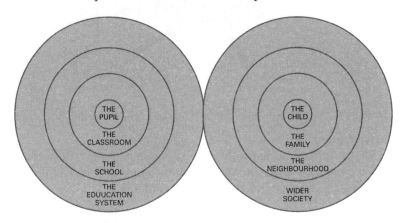

Figure 10.10 A concentric ring diagram used here to think about the different sources of influence on students' examination results

THE PUPIL
THE CLASSROOM
THE SCHOOL
THE EDUUCATION SYSTEM

THE CHILD
THE FAMILY
THE NEIGHBOURHOOD
WIDER SOCIETY

Figure 10.11 A pyramid diagram used here to think about the structure of an organization

Managing Director
Senior Manager
Plant Managers
Supervisors
Assembly workers

Figure 10.12 A map diagram used here to think about where particular kinds of behaviour occur. This relates to the café research mentioned earlier

ON STAGE
The public area of the café. Staff in full view of customers showing their 'public face' to customers.

Dining area
Facing customers at counter or till.

ON-STAGE/OFF-STAGE BOUNDARY
Staff can give each other secret messages about customers – at counter/at kitchen door

OFF STAGE
Only staff in view and in communication with each other.

In kitchen and in staff rest area.

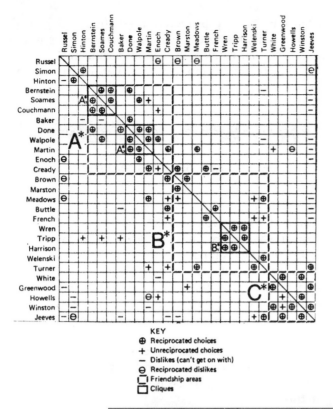

KEY
⊕ Reciprocated choices
\+ Unreciprocated choices
− Dislikes (can't get on with)
⊖ Reciprocated dislikes
⊏⊐ Friendship areas
▢ Cliques

Figure 10.13 A sociometric grid drawn from data collected by asking students to name their best friends. It shows who chose who and was or was not chosen in return. Figure 8 from Lacey, C. (1970) Hightown Grammar, Manchester University Press

	Female students	Male students
Lessons involving technological equipment	**A** Hang back in using equipment. Chat more than in C.	**B** Are quick to monopolize equipment. Are more engaged than in D.
Lessons not involving technological equipment	**C** Take leading role in these lessons.	**D** Are less cooperative than females in these lessons.

Figure 10.14 A 2 × 2 grid used here to think about the reasons for gender differences in student behaviour

Remember, all the techniques are introduced here only as ways of helping you to identify patterns in your data. You still have the final task of writing up your findings in a report. With your key points arranged, you can decide on a writing order.

Providing evidence for your key points

When introducing each of the key points in your report, you will have to refer to your collection of original data and evidence. Some of your evidence will be summarized in your own words; some will be expressed in the exact words of the people you have talked to. You may choose to quote some of these direct items of evidence; this will certainly add credibility to your descriptions and conclusions. However, these quotations must be completely accurate and you should identify the speaker, the date and the occasion.

► You may choose not to use real names to identify your speakers. You may want to respect confidentiality.

Do not fall into the trap of merely presenting a long string of quotations. If you do, the reader will feel that you have not made any sense of your data. Think of quotations as illustrating and reinforcing the main stream of your report, rather than as making up the report itself.

BEFORE YOU FINALIZE YOUR CONCLUSIONS

Finally, here are some questions to answer before you complete your report.

- Go back to your stated objectives or hypotheses. What did you set out to do? Have you done it?
- Look again at what others have written. How does your research and findings compare with theirs?
- Ask some fellow students or perhaps tutors to read the last draft of your report. Give them enough evidence to help them to decide whether your interpretations appear correct or valid. What is their response? How can you improve your arguments?

▶ Do not expect that everyone will agree with what you have written!

- Compare data that you have collected in different ways and from different people or places. Does it seem to be consistent? This checking process is sometimes called **triangulation**.

▶ See Chapter 5, p. 78.

- Sometimes you may be able to go back to the people in your sample to see how much *they* agree with your findings. You may then want to change what you have written or at least to report their reactions. This sharing of data with them can also be a way of thanking them for being involved in the research.
- Get your tutor or other colleagues to give an opinion on whether they would have been likely to record the same data if they had been in similar situations. The question here is: 'How reliable is the data?'
- Look for other ways of explaining your findings. Could there be another very different explanation? For instance, a biologist viewed the movement of some larvae and noted that they moved from a light area into a dark area. His explanation was that they preferred the dark. But he had to agree that there were other possible explanations: the larvae may have preferred a cooler area, or perhaps they were merely playing follow-my-leader.
- Think about the part *you* have played in the project. How much do you think *you* have influenced the situation? Have you been as unbiased as possible? Did you set out with certain assumptions that influenced your judgements? Have you taken things for granted that you should have questioned?

The main criteria for judging research

 Now turn back to the section headed 'Criteria for judging research' in Chapter 4 (pp. 54–7) and ask yourself the following questions about your research:

1 How reliable were my methods?
2 How representative was what I studied? What generalizations can I make?
3 How valid were my conclusions?
4 How objective was my research?

and looking at the notes you made in Chapter 2:

5 How ethically correct was my research?

You will need to answer all these questions when you write up your project.

▶ Writing up is dealt with in Chapter 11.

FURTHER READING

You may need to go more deeply into statistical testing, in which case you need to find additional books that concentrate on that. Two books that are relatively easy to follow are:

Coolican, H. (1993) *Research Methods and Statistics in Psychology* (2nd edn), Sevenoaks: Hodder & Stoughton.
Maglennon, K. (1993) *Essential Practical Psychology*, London: Collins Educational.

Although these are both psychology books, what they tell you about statistics can easily be applied to other topics.

If you want to read more about qualitative data there are lots of useful ideas in a book by Judith Riley:

Riley, J. (1990) *Getting the Most from Your Data: A Handbook of Practical Ideas on How to Analyse Qualitative Data*, Technical and Educational Services.

CHAPTER SUMMARY

In this chapter we have looked at:

• ways of arranging your data so that you can look for patterns and draw conclusions;
• ways of presenting data to make it easy for a reader to understand.

(11) *Writing up*

Chapter objectives
By the end of this chapter you will be able to:

▌ plan the structure of your report;

▌ use the appropriate conventions in writing up your report;

▌ check, polish and evaluate your report;

▌ evaluate what you have learned from doing research.

WRITING UP AS YOU GO ALONG

It is tempting to think of writing up as something you do after the active and 'real work' of gathering your research data is complete and hence as something you leave to the end of your project. If you adopt this attitude you will miss out on opportunities to think critically about your work while it is under way. The process of writing can help to clarify your thinking on an issue and could stimulate new trains of thought. Writing from an early stage also gets you used to the process and makes the overall task less daunting. So get into the habit of writing at all stages of your project rather than leaving it to the end.

What you write during the course of the research does not have to be in its final 'polished' state. The important thing is to start writing so that this becomes an integral part of your project, and so that you have plenty of material in draft form when you come to write up your final version of the report. If you are using a research notebook you could divide it into sections that reflect the structure of your report. You can then record your results, ideas and observations under the appropriate headings as they happen. Some writers use a ring-binder and write one paragraph on one side of each sheet of paper. This makes it easy to reorder the material if necessary.

Whichever approach you adopt you will need to plan the structure of your report at a very early stage of your project.

PLANNING THE STRUCTURE OF YOUR REPORT

The structure of a research report may appear very rigid but it is important to stick to the conventions. The purpose of reporting research is to communicate results to an audience. A research report is not a continuous narrative but an arrangement of information. If the information is laid out in a standard form, with clear headings and structure, then readers should be able to discover quickly what they want to know about a piece of research.

It may be that you have been told which headings to use in your report. In some cases they will have been made explicit in a title you have been given. If this is the case then, obviously, you follow the instructions. If not, there are conventions for reporting research, described below, which should be generally applicable to your research, though clearly not every report will fit this pattern exactly. If you have not been given a prescribed format for your report, the format outlined below is a useful guide which you can modify and adapt for your own purposes.

► Sometimes you will be provided with a format for your final report.

► If you have not been given a format for your report, try amending this format to fit your needs.

Basic structure for a research report

1 Title
The title should reflect the specific problem or question being asked and give some indication of your approach. Check that the title is still accurate when you have finished writing your report.

2 Contents
A table of contents is required for longer reports. It should list the names of chapters or sections of the report, with the page number on which each begins.

3 Abstract
You must include a synopsis of your report which, when read in conjunction with the title, should help the reader to decide whether to read the whole report. Abstracts are always required for reports that are going to be published. It is also a good idea to provide an abstract if your report is an assessed part of your course, because it makes the job of assessors and verifiers easier.

4 Introduction
The introduction should state, in more detail than the title, the specific problem or question under consideration. The purpose (i.e. aims) and scope of your research should be stated clearly. A fairly brief general statement of the background to the problem, to give the setting of the investigation and point out its importance, should also be included. This is also the place to define the terms you are going to use. This section should be straightforward and brief, the intention being to enable a reader to find out precisely what the research project involved.

5 Literature survey
The literature survey is a review of previous work that you have studied. Ideally it should be a discussion of selected research studies showing that your work is sensible and worthwhile in its field and explaining how it relates to earlier work. References to sources used are conventionally given by adding the date in brackets after the author's name, or by giving author and date in brackets.

► See 'Bibliographies and references', pp. 164–5.

6 Method

The method section describes what research you did and how you went about it. You should go into enough detail to enable readers to repeat the research you undertook if they choose to do so. The following items might appear, depending of course on the nature of your project:

- an introductory statement outlining the reasons for your choice of research methods (unless this has already been covered in your introduction);
- a list of any apparatus or equipment used (or a diagram);
- the conditions and procedures of any experiments and observations;
- the sources of secondary information that you relied on and any sampling and control devices used;
- the measurement techniques used;
- your reasons for selecting a particular method if there were alternatives;
- a description of any participants or subjects used in your research.

7 Results

You will need to have a section that states the results of your research. Often, it will be in the form of tables or graphs derived from an analysis of the data you have recorded. The text in this section takes the form of a linking commentary. This is not the place to include a discussion of, or to draw inferences from, your findings or observations; this is a strictly factual and descriptive section.

8 Discussion

In the discussion section you can analyse your findings and observations, making interpretations and judgements. It is probably the hardest section of all to write because it is difficult to know what to include. Perhaps the surest guide is to concentrate on quality rather than quantity. Your readers will appreciate it if you are not long-winded. You should aim to:

- interpret the results;
- show their significance and how they add to existing knowledge;
- discuss your project in relation to theories underlying any similar research;
- refer to the aims that you stated in the introduction and consider whether you have met them;
- discuss the precision of your results;
- explain any discrepancies or unexpected results (which themselves may be significant);
- compare your results with the findings of any studies you cited in your literature survey.

The information in a carefully considered and well-written discussion should enable readers to judge the validity of your conclusions.

9 Conclusions

You should then make a brief statement of the conclusions that can justifiably be drawn from your research. This section should not be another summary of your results. If the results of your research are inconclusive, you should state this and explain why. It may also be appropriate to include suggestions for future work.

10 Recommendations

If the research is of the kind that collects information on which future decisions could be based, your report may need a list of recommendations. These should:

- be numbered;
- be cross-referenced to the parts of the report that give rise to the recommendation;
- be addressed to someone, or some agency in particular: for example, 'Recommendations to the Personnel Manager' (make sure these are the appropriate people for your recommendations);
- be carefully phrased to show what action is recommended – if you are recommending that something be discussed, say 'to consider'; if you are recommending that action be taken, use a 'doing' word;
- indicate either a time for action or a priority of importance.

11 References

You should provide a list of references actually cited in the text of your report but do not include all the literature you have consulted. Present the list in alphabetical order. The convention is that a book is described by author, initials, date, title, place of publication, publisher. A journal article is described by author, initials, date, title of article, title of journal, volume (and issue) number, page numbers.

► See pp. 164–5.

12 Appendices

Copies of any research instruments you have used (such as questionnaires, interview schedules and diagrams of scientific apparatus) should be included as appendices and referred to in the main body of the text. Unless illustrative material is brief, or is an integral part of the section presented, graphs, statistics, lists and so on are also best presented in appendices to the report, where they may be referred to when required.

You may also be asked to provide a separate **evaluation** section giving an objective appraisal of the strengths and weaknesses of your project.

Note on scientific reports

The conventions for scientific reports are not quite the same as those given above and are very specific. If you are writing a scientific report ask your tutor's advice about what exactly is expected.

► For this activity refer also to the assessment specifications for your project. Find out which sections of the report will carry the most marks.

PRESENTATION

Schools, colleges, universities and examination boards will generally give you information on how your finished report should be presented. This will cover points such as the size of paper to be used (usually A4), what kind of file or ring-binder to use, how and where your name and the title of the course should appear, and so on. The finished report should be tidy and well presented but, unless there are marks allotted for presentation, don't spend a lot of time and money on fancy colour-work, illustrations or bindings.

The structure of your report

You may have been given an outline structure to work from, or you may use an amended version of the structure given earlier in this chapter. In either case, write down each heading you think you will be using on a separate sheet of paper. Then after each heading write:

Here I should. . .

and note down what you think you should include in each section. Take your finished notes to a tutor and ask whether these notes form an adequate plan for your report. Once you have these headings settled, you can set up a file with file spacers – one for each section of the report. Each headed page, with its notes, then becomes a working document on which to base each section.

Order of writing

It is unlikely that the readers of your report will start at the beginning and read through to the end. Similarly, when you are writing your report you may not necessarily start with the introduction. Often the review of previous work can be written first and the section on the methods used can be drafted at an early stage. It is up to you to decide which order and method of writing suits you best.

Remember, however, to draft the aims and scope of your project at an early stage and refer to this draft frequently throughout your research to ensure that what you are doing is still relevant to your line of enquiry. An abstract or summary should be written last of all since you cannot summarize properly until the whole report is before you.

Style and expression

Use the clearest and simplest language that the material allows. Be as brief as you can while at the same time supplying sufficient information, and remember to keep your readers' interest. Don't include more than one idea in each sentence. Use short paragraphs. Make specific and concrete points wherever possible and avoid vague generalizations and abstract points. Eliminate unnecessary words. Strive to be as objective as possible: leave out personal comments such as: 'I think the experiment was very successful'. An effective way of achieving an objective feel to a written report is to use the third person and the passive voice rather than the first person and the active voice, for example: 'The sample was taken from a cross-section of the population,' rather than 'I took a sample from a cross-section of the population.'

Grammar, spelling and punctuation

You will find it much easier to write up your research if you have a sound knowledge of grammar, spelling and punctuation. Poorly expressed, ungrammatical and badly spelt work will detract from the quality of your research. It is disappointing if potentially sound research findings are dismissed for these reasons. Ask for help from your tutor if you have problems with these skills. There may be a communications workshop at your college, with specialist help available. If you think you need help with your written English, ask your tutor what is available.

▶ Read your work aloud to yourself or into a tape recorder and check the grammar and punctuation of any sections that do not flow smoothly.

Layout

Guidelines on layout may be available for your course. If not, then the following guidelines are generally acceptable.

The report should be clearly written, typed or word-processed, with generous margins and lots of 'white space' on the page. Some schools, colleges and universities require that reports be typed or word-processed (and you may be able to gain IT grades for doing your own word-processing). Type using double line-spacing to make reading and marking easier. Number all the pages and type or write on one side of the page only. Include attractive and relevant graphics where possible. Again, using a computer software package will help with this and may gain you some IT marks.

Page, section and paragraph numbering

You must always number your pages. If your report is going to contain many cross-references, it will be helpful if, in addition, you number each subsection or each paragraph as well. The usual convention for numbering is to number each major section, and then each subsection or paragraph. Thus for (major) Section 2, the first subsection will be 2.1. Be consistent in your use of Arabic (1, 2, 3, 4, . . .) or Roman (i, ii, iii, iv, . . .) numerals; and lower case (a, b, c, d, . . .) or upper case (A, B, C, D, . . .) letters.

Academic conventions

Academic writing and reading follow certain standard conventions that are helpful for both writer and reader. Many of the conventions stem from reporting on research where the reader needs to be able to follow up references in order to understand fully or to evaluate the research. Different academic disciplines have their own variations of the standard conventions.

The most obvious variations you may notice as you read around your subject area are in the format for a bibliography or reference entry. Most educational institutions will have a preferred style and will offer guidance about how referencing is to be done. Check with your tutor about which style you are expected to follow in writing your report. Some tutors have personal preferences that they will want you to adopt. Whichever style you adopt, take care to use it consistently and accurately throughout your report.

Bibliographies and references

► The British system and the Harvard system are the most commonly used approaches for listing references and bibliographies.

Strictly speaking, a bibliography is a full list of all material written about a given area. Thus bibliographies are sometimes books in themselves. A bibliography in relation to writing up research is usually defined as a list of sources consulted during the preparation of a project. Opinions vary about whether project reports need to have a bibliography of this kind and/or a list of references. The difference between the two is that references give specific details of particular books or articles that have been cited or referred to in the report, whereas a bibliography is a list of works you have consulted during your research, whether or not you refer to them in your report. You need to consult your tutor about what is expected. Two approaches to referencing and preparing bibliographies are in common use, namely the British system and the Harvard system.

The British system

The British system places the author's initials before the surname, and the date appears after the publisher (for books) and after the volume, part or issue number (for journals), as follows:

P. Thompson, *The Edwardians: The Remaking of British Society*, London, Weidenfeld & Nicholson (1984).
P. Wilkinson, 'English Youth Movements 1908–70', *Journal of Contemporary History*, vol. 4, no. 2 (1969), pp. 12–13.

The disadvantage of this method is that when works are referred to in the main body of the text, references have to be supplied by means of either footnotes or endnotes. For example, in the main text, 'P. Thompson, in his discussion of the social history of Edwardian Britain[1] . . . ', and in a footnote or at the end of a chapter,

1   P. Thompson, *The Edwardians: The Remaking of British Society*, London, Weidenfeld & Nicholson (1984).

The Harvard system

The Harvard system places the author's surname before the initials and the date immediately after the author's name as in the following examples:

Thompson, P. (1984), *The Edwardians: The Remaking of British Society*, London, Weidenfeld & Nicholson.
Wilkinson, P. (1969), 'English Youth Movements 1908–70', *Journal of Contemporary History* 4(2): 12–13.

The Harvard system is preferable to the British system because it avoids footnotes and endnotes, which can interrupt the flow of the text, while still ensuring that adequate information about sources is provided. The convention is that in the text, the author's surname, the date of publication and the page reference are included, for example, 'As Thompson (1984, p. 20) says . . . ', or just '(Thompson 1984: 20)'. The full details of Thompson's 1984 publication will then appear in the alphabetical list of references at the end of the report. Page references should be given in the text where material is directly quoted or is heavily drawn upon.

Sources appear in alphabetical order at the end of the report, not in the order in which they appear in the text. If the author has more than one entry, then the publications are listed in chronological order of publication. If the author has published more than one work in a particular year, the different works are labelled: a, b, c, etc.: for example: Thompson 1984a, Thompson 1984b.

When you have selected a method of referencing (or been advised which to use), remember to be consistent throughout. It also pays to establish good habits very early on in your research. When you record a source, use the format of your chosen system including the correct punctuation (see the model index cards in Chapter 9, Figure 9.7). If your index cards are in good order it is a comparatively easy task to produce your references or a bibliography. All you have to do is sort your cards into alphabetical order and present them as a list at the end of your report.

Quotations

Direct quotations from sources are used:

- to illustrate a point;
- to add an extra dimension to your argument;
- to express an idea succinctly;
- to give the general flavour of a piece of work;
- where the words, not just ideas, of an author are under discussion;
- if an author's apt style cannot readily be conveyed acceptably in your own words.

Presentation of quotations

Short quotations (only a few words or one sentence) should be set between quotation marks in the main text, with the source in brackets (if using the Harvard system) or with a footnote (if using the British system). If you deliberately miss words out of the quotation, show this by including three full stops (an ellipsis). For example: **As Gombrich (1984: 19) says, 'If we take art to mean such activities as building temples and houses . . . there is no people in all the world without art.'**

Long quotations (longer than around thirty words) should be set apart from the main body of the text and indented. For example: **As Gombrich (1984: 19) says,**

> We do not know how art began any more than we know how language started. If we take art to mean such activities as building temples and houses, making pictures and sculptures, or weaving patterns, there is no people in all the world without art.

► Record the sources of quotations at the same time as you copy out the quotation.

PLAGIARISM

Plagiarism means passing off someone else's thoughts or writing as if they were your own. It is unacceptable to copy from a source without acknowledging that source. This includes not only direct quotations but also paraphrasing someone else's work (re-expressing it in your own words) without acknowledging it. Most tutors are able to spot a case of plagiarism quite easily because they are familiar with the sources you are likely to use. Extreme forms of plagiarism, such as copying another student's work or an entire journal article or chapter from a book, are cheating and can have serious consequences for you. Not only may you fail the piece of assessment but in some cases disciplinary action may be taken.

To avoid plagiarism
When taking notes:

* express the material in your own words;
* clearly identify the beginning and end of any paraphrases;
* if you copy a piece exactly, put it in quotation marks;
* note the source, including the page numbers.

When writing up:

* put direct quotations in quotation marks;
* use references (Harvard system) or footnotes/endnotes (British system) to acknowledge the source.

EDITING AND REVISING YOUR DRAFT

No one can write a research report straight off and produce the finished article in one go. You must be prepared to draft, redraft and redraft at least once more until you are satisfied with the end result. When planning the writing up of your report, always allow plenty of time for editing, revision and rewriting. In your planning timetable allow for a few days between drafts if possible. This will help you to look at your work with new eyes and evaluate it afresh. It is easy to acquire tunnel vision when working solidly on something, and it is difficult to be objective about material that you have read too often.

Producing your report on a word-processor greatly reduces the time and effort involved in redrafting, but creates the temptation to go on revising for too long. You will have to compromise somewhere.

Check your work section by section for accuracy and appropriateness to the task. Does it follow a logical sequence and make sense? Is there a clear argument? Is there any ambiguity? Does the report serve the purpose for which it was intended? Have you kept the reader in mind in presenting the report? It is particularly important to check:

* spelling,
* grammar,
* punctuation,
* referencing,
* quotations.

When you believe you have achieved your final draft, try to get someone else to read and check your work for you. If this is not possible, try reading your report aloud. This should pick up any awkward phrases, mistakes in grammar, incorrect use of tenses and so on.

▶ Have you allowed enough time for writing up? If you suspect you have not, amend the time and action plan you produced in Chapter 7.

WRITING AN ABSTRACT

For a really professional finish to your written report you should prepare an abstract, which is a synopsis of the content of your report. The abstract can be presented before the main body of your report and enables the reader to find out quickly the nature and outcomes of your research. Writing an abstract is also a further way of checking that the title of your research is accurate. In Chapter 3 you were urged to revisit continually the defining of the subject and title of your research. Even after the project is written up it is not too late to change the title if, after you have summarized the content, you find that the title does not correspond accurately to the report you have written.

Writing a good abstract is quite difficult. The skill lies in knowing what to leave out while retaining the essence of what your research is about. The major elements of your report should provide the skeleton of the abstract, i.e. introduction, method, results, discussion and conclusions. Remember, it is not detail that is needed here but the bare bones of what you aimed to do and why, where it fits in with other research, how you did it, what the results were and what conclusions can be drawn.

► If you are doing a GNVQ course, make sure that you are familiar with the 'grading criteria', especially those concerned with evaluation.

EVALUATING YOUR RESEARCH

When you believe you have finally produced the definitive version of your report you may feel that your task is over. However, for the audience of your report, be it your tutor, other students or whoever, the task of evaluating what you have achieved has just begun. Those looking at your work will be judging it against a set of criteria. While the criteria will vary for different types of research, there are some questions that should be asked of any type of research. It is a good idea to subject your own work to the sort of rigorous questioning it is likely to face from others.

Evaluation checklist

Does the title reflect the nature of your research?

Does the abstract (if any) give a clear idea of what is in the report?

Are the aims and objectives clearly stated?

Have you achieved them?

Are any hypotheses proved or not proved?

Are all the terms used clearly defined?

Is the report well written, its meaning clear, with no ambiguities or irrelevant or obscure sections? Have you checked and rechecked spelling, grammar, punctuation and tenses, and have you eliminated all colloquialisms.

Have all the sources you have used been referenced?

Have you studied an adequate amount of literature relating to your research?

Does the literature review (if any) place your research into the context of the area of study as a whole?

Are your methods of data collection accurately described? Are they appropriate to the aims of your research? Have you explained why you chose them?

Have you analysed and interpreted the data rather than merely described it?

Are the results clearly presented with appropriate use of graphs, tables, diagrams, etc.?

Are your conclusions based on evidence?

Is there any evidence of bias? Have you used any subjective or emotive language?

How reliable is the data?

Are any recommendations realistically achievable?

Have you acknowledged any limitations to your research?

Have you taken into account any ethical considerations?

If you can answer all the above questions satisfactorily then you are ready to make your final copy of the report. If the report is typed, especially by someone else, make sure you check it for errors before handing it in.

Of course, the results of your research may not be what you

anticipated when you embarked on the project. Indeed, you may feel that you have 'failed'. Do not be downcast if the results of your research are not what you expected. Do please remember that student research is judged as much by what the student has learned from doing the research as by the quality of the research. So an important part of evaluating your research is to reflect not only on the research itself but on your experience and what you learned from it. The list of questions below will help you to evaluate what the research process has taught you and what you have put into it. This exercise can only be of value if you are honest with yourself!

► **Viva voce examinations:** If your assessment includes a viva voce (oral) examination then make sure you read your report thoroughly before the oral. Try to read it as your assessor might read it, spotting the kinds of questions the assessor might ask. Make sure you can answer the questions.

What have I learned from my research?

- What were my aims and objectives when I began my research?
- What were my strengths in relation to those aims and objectives?
- What were my weaknesses?
- Did I make use of my strengths?
- How did I try to overcome any weaknesses?
- How much reading did I do (quantity and quality)?
- Was the amount of reading I did too little or too much, too shallow or too detailed?
- What was the quality of my note-taking? Did I record all references accurately? Could I retrieve information easily?
- What did I learn from the methodologies I used?
- What did I learn from my experience of writing up my research?
- What did I learn from things that did not go according to plan?
- What did I learn from working with other people?
- What did I learn about myself and my ability to undertake research?
- Have I learned anything about myself that I will be able to use in other areas of my life?

CHAPTER SUMMARY

In this chapter we have given you advice on how to write up a final report. We have suggested that:

- you regard writing up as something you do throughout your project – not just at the end;
- you plan your report carefully, taking into consideration the conventions you are required to follow;
- you avoid plagiarism;
- you take care in preparing, drafting, finalizing and presenting your report;
- you use your report to review and evaluate what you have learned from doing the research.

(12) Giving an oral presentation

Chapter objectives
After working through this chapter you will be able to:

▌ plan and deliver an oral presentation;

▌ take part in a group presentation;

▌ plan, deliver and lead a seminar;

▌ take part in a discussion;

▌ evaluate your performance.

THE IMPORTANCE OF ORAL PRESENTATION SKILLS

You may not be making a formal oral presentation of the results of your research. However, many programmes of study recognize the importance of good oral communication skills, and tutors often create opportunities for oral presentations within the courses they teach. In GNVQ courses, oral presentations by individuals or by groups are often required as part of the assessment package and also feature in Communication core skills. Such presentations take varied forms, for instance:

- a presentation to a group of people about the research you propose to do;
- an oral interim report or summary of how your research is going;
- a formal presentation to your tutor or assessor, perhaps in the form of a 'viva' in which you explain and evaluate your research findings as part of the assessment process;
- a seminar paper or mini-lecture to fellow students, followed by leading a discussion;
- a role-play exercise where points of view have to be argued and defended.

Oral presentations are widely used in the business world, especially when presenting new ideas or when trying to sell a product or service. Many employers include a presentation as part of the process of selecting new staff.

The prospect of giving an oral presentation often causes considerable alarm. By careful preparation and practice, however, anyone can learn to communicate well with an audience. There may even come a time when you can look forward to such an experience.

Of course, practice alone doesn't necessarily improve perfor-

▶ The key words are **preparation** and **practice**.

mance. By practising, critically reflecting on your performance and getting constructive feedback from your tutors, your audience and your friends, you will get the information that will help you to improve. The emphasis should be on constructive feedback – because you need to know what you are doing well and how to improve what you are doing badly. You also need to nurture your self-confidence, which is an essential component of verbal communication. So when you have prepared your talk, try it out first on a willing listener, someone whose judgement you value. From this audience of one, work up to a small group, and so on. We shall come back to practice later on, but now let's look at how to prepare for an oral presentation.

GIVING A FORMAL PRESENTATION

In preparing and giving a presentation you are attempting to communicate information to other people.

 Kinds of oral communication

Make a list of everyday situations where you orally communicate information to other people. These might include:

- giving directions to a stranger to your town;
- telling a friend the plot of a book, film or television programme;
- explaining how to get to the next level in a computer game;
- asking for something in a shop;
- explaining why you were late for an appointment;
- describing the new shopping precinct in a telephone call to a friend who has moved away.

Some of these activities require a creative approach; some require precise attention to detail. What they all require is for the communicator to have some knowledge and understanding of what he or she is describing, explaining, telling, giving or asking for.

The same is true of more formal situations. You must have something to say and be interested in saying it. Being able to make what you are communicating interesting and understandable is very important if you are to hold the attention of your audience. If your presentation is to be assessed by your tutors, you will have two more aims:

▶ You must have something to say, and be interested in saying it.

1 to demonstrate that you have a good grasp of the subject matter;
2 to demonstrate the quality of your oral presentation skills.

For the first of these, you should be very clear about how much you are expected to know and in how much detail. Check this with your tutor. For the second of these aims, you should know how these

► For GNVQ students, this is included in the Core Skills criteria.

skills are going to be assessed. If necessary, ask your tutor for a copy of the criteria that he or she will use to assess your performance.

Preparation

To help you plan what you are going to say and to prepare yourself to say it, the following areas need to be considered:

- knowing your audience and adopting an appropriate style;
- identifying aims and objectives;
- developing a structure to the talk;
- choosing visual aids;
- being aware of non-verbal communication;
- practising the presentation;
- structuring the physical environment;
- identifying strategies for evaluation.

Knowing your audience

Media companies spend millions of pounds each year investigating the likes, dislikes, whims and fancies of their perceived audience. Audiences differ, and spending some time evaluating your potential audience will help you to tailor your talk appropriately, produce effective visual aids and devise evaluation strategies. It is not necessarily easier to give a talk to a group of people you know well. It may be less stressful to talk to a community group or a group of students from another year or course. Time spent in researching your audience will help you to control your nervousness since you will be better prepared and therefore more confident and the situation should then become less alarming.

 Work through the following checklist.

Is your audience:
(a) other students from your group? ☐
(b) students from a different group? ☐
(c) a group of individuals from outside your
    school/college whom you already know? ☐
(d) a group of individuals from outside your
    school/college whom you don't know? ☐

Are they familiar with the subject matter? ☐
How large is the group?

```

```

Where will you give the talk?

```

```

Can you rearrange the room if necessary? ☐

What facilities are available – e.g. overhead projector, blackboard, white board, video equipment, tape cassette player, slide projector, other?

For how long should you talk?

What do you want your audience to learn from your talk?

If your audience falls into the (a) or (b) category:
Are you all giving a talk to the group in turns?   ☐
Have your tutors given you guidelines on the format of the talk?   ☐
Are you speaking about a subject that is known to the group? ☐
If not, will you need to provide handouts prior to the talk?   ☐

If your group falls into the (c) or (d) category:
What is the age range of your audience?

How much do they know about your subject?

Why are you giving the talk (have they asked you to or have you asked to talk to them)?

Once you have established what sort of audience you have, you can start to plan your presentation.

Style

Oral communication, even more than written communication, is a social activity. Spoken exchanges between people exist in a social context, and are both a cause and an effect of the relationship between the sender and receiver. Within the communicated message is the communicator's implied intention, which should be picked up by the receiver. This doesn't always happen. There are plenty of examples of mis-communication, when people 'get the wrong end of the stick'. In a formal situation, it is therefore important to make your intentions, your aims, explicit to your audience.

The social context of the communication will affect the type of language used and the way it is said. For example, telling a friend the plot of a film would probably involve lots of incomplete sentences, gestures, a discussion of the various merits of this or that

► Telling your audience what you are going to say, and why, is usually a good idea.

► Adjust your style to the situation.

actor, who you went to the film with, what you did on the way home and so on. If you were asked to describe the plot of the same film to a tutor or to a group of students, you would probably phrase your description in a more formal manner, sticking to the plot, giving a list of actors and characterization. The event you were describing would be the same, but the style you used would be different because of the different context and expectations.

 Using a video recorder, record the following examples of different styles of speech from the television:

- a newscaster;
- a 'talking heads' type of television programme – Question Time might be a good example;
- a documentary or fly-on-the-wall type of programme.

Compare the different styles of presentation, particularly in terms of formality and informality, and of how polished the performance is.

You probably found that the newscaster gave a very polished performance; remember that he or she was probably using an Autocue – an electronic aid placed beside the camera that enables broadcasters to read their script while looking at the camera.

Considerable care, attention and skill will have gone into writing the script, and newscasters are practised in voice intonation, clarity and expression so that what they read is understandable and interesting.

The more 'live' type of television show, even if it features politicians and other well-practised public speakers, will probably display a more naturalistic style of speech, interruptions, jokes, gestures and so on.

The documentary or 'fly-on-the-wall' programme gives a more accurate representation of the way we usually speak to one another, though even this will have been edited and selected by the director. In this casual, everyday style of speech, you will find unfinished sentences, sprinkled with 'ers' and 'ums', overlapping speech and interruptions. However, what is being communicated is usually understood by the receiver. Human beings are very good at guessing meaning from speech, making sense of the whole interrelationship of words with intonation, gestures, facial expressions, sighs, giggles and so on.

For a presentation of research you will need to be fairly formal in your style of presentation.

Identifying aims and objectives

You may be asked to give a presentation on a subject of your own choice. On the other hand, you may be required to present a 'snapshot' of where you have reached with your research. Perhaps you are to give a final presentation of your whole research project. In each case, you will have to clarify the aims and objectives of the presentation and ensure that you stick to the time you have been given. If you have done your research and know your subject well, you will have too much material and you will have to concentrate on communicating just a few main points.

Ask yourself:

> What is the main thing that I want to get across to my audience?

▶ What are the main points to get across to your audience?

For example, suppose you have been asked to give a talk on the following topic:

> How playing helps the social development of pre-school children.

The aim of your talk will vary depending on the nature of your audience. If the audience is made up of members of the local branch of the Pre-School Playgroups Association, you can rely on their having some sympathy for what you are going to say and some common understanding of the subject. They will want to take away some practical ideas from your talk and you should plan it with this in mind. If, however, your audience consists of the other students in your group, they may not have much experience of this subject, and their main aim may be to learn enough to pass a test. In this case, you should present some basic information in a clear and well-organized way.

Having established your aim, and related this aim to your intended audience, you will need to identify exactly what you want your audience to have learned from your talk. These learning outcomes or objectives should be written in a form that can be assessed. This will be discussed later under the heading of: 'Strategies for evaluation'.

▶ Your **aim** is the overall purpose of your talk; your **objectives** are the components of this aim. Think of your aim as the end point of your talk and your objectives as the steps on the way to this.

In listing objectives it is helpful to use active verbs that lead to actions that can be evaluated, for example:

> At the end of my talk the audience should be able to:
>
> - **recognize** stages of social development in pre-school children, and/or
> - **link** stages of social development with play activities, and/or
> - **identify** types of play activities to use with children who are experiencing behaviour difficulties.

These are your objectives.

If you wanted your audience to **understand the importance** of play you might find it difficult to measure whether you had achieved this objective, since all members of the audience would presumably have to take some test or exam in order to prove that they had indeed understood.

Setting a testable objective

Let's try another example. The aim is to introduce the audience to conducting oral histories as a research method. Can you identify some learning objectives?

These are the objectives that we came up with:

At the end of the talk the audience should be able to:

- explain what an 'oral history' is;
- identify the skills involved in conducting oral history research;
- identify issues of validity in using oral histories as a research method.

Link your objectives with your evaluation methods
Title of talk:

The aim(s) I have for this talk are:

1
2

The objectives I have for this talk are:

1
2
3
4
5, etc.

At the end of my talk I intend the audience to be able to:

A
B
C
D

(The extent to which you have achieved your objectives can then be evaluated against the audience's grasp of points A, B, C, D, etc.)

▶ Unless you set objectives for your presentation, and can determine whether these objectives have been achieved, you will be unable to evaluate your performance.

Developing a structure to the talk

Once you have established your aims and objectives, it is a relatively simple task to give a structure to your talk. You may wish to refer to the previous chapter, which discussed how to plan and structure a written report. When planning an oral presentation you should establish three clear areas:

▶ This list is a variant on the old adage of 'Tell 'em what you're going to tell 'em; tell 'em; tell 'em what you've told 'em.'

1 introduction,
2 body of work,
3 conclusion.

The introduction should set out a clear framework for the talk and the conclusion should summarize the main points made in the body of the talk.

If this is your first presentation, you may feel more comfortable in writing out your talk like an essay. However, there is nothing more boring for an audience than listening to someone reading out something that he or she has written earlier. So by all means write your talk out like an essay, but then rework it into a framework that is suitable for being delivered orally.

Key words

Now let's think of a structure that would help us achieve the objectives set out on p. 176. One way to approach the task is to identify key words, since you would need to define these key words as part of a talk. Key words here would be **social development**; **play activities**; **behaviour difficulties**. Part of the structure of your talk would therefore be to define these terms. However, your overall aim is to explore how playing helps the social development of pre-school children and you will therefore need to provide clear links between these key terms to support the development of this argument. So the framework could begin to develop like this:

Define: Pre-school children's social development; stages of development.
Define: Play activities – what are they, how might they help social development?
Define: Behaviour difficulties – what are they; how could play help children overcome such difficulties?

Examples

Having established a framework you can begin to note down your main ideas under headings such as those above. You will probably find that using index cards (6 × 4 inches) is a good way to keep your notes clear and accessible (and stop you writing out an essay!).

Number your cards. Note one main component (think of it as being like a paragraph) on each card and add your supporting ideas. These cards will act as prompts and ensure that you don't forget a key point when giving your talk. Using an index card prompt system will help you to talk to your audience and not read a set text.

Once you have developed the structure of your talk and communicated this structure to your audience in your introduction, you need to keep emphasizing key points that you make during the talk. Audiences do not have the benefit of being able to flip back through a previous section if they get lost; it is up to you to ensure they understand what is going on. Signposting the way in which your argument is going, by giving short reminders during the talk, is a useful way to keep your audience with you. For example:

> 'Having explored the key stages of social development in pre-school children with you, I shall now go on to consider what play activities help children's social development.'

'To recap, the main types of play activities engaged in by young children are: . . . '

In this way you will ensure that you keep to the structure of your talk and that your audience is clear about what you are trying to achieve.

Choosing visual aids

Visual aids can be very helpful when you are giving a talk. If they show the main points you are making, they can act both as a prompt to you and as the basis for the audience to make notes. A visual aid can present a diagram of a process that you could never describe clearly in words. Visual aids encourage the audience to use their sense of sight as well as hearing, which helps them to concentrate. But do be careful to leave enough time for your audience to study, read and understand what you are showing them. It is very easy to remove a visual aid before people have finished reading it, let alone understood it.

Some visual aids you may be able to use include:

- overhead projector (OHP),
- slide projector,
- large maps mounted on display boards,
- large photographs mounted on display boards,
- working or static models,
- video clips,
- flip charts/blackboards/white boards.

There are entire books available on using visual aids, but here are just a few general tips:

1 Make sure that the seats are arranged so that everyone can see the visual display easily.
2 A slide projector has to be used in semi-darkness, so your audience cannot read or take notes while watching.
3 Slides should be loaded and ready before your talk begins. Check that they are in the right order, the right way round and the right way up.
4 Make sure that you have a spare bulb, spare leads and access to a technician if anything breaks down.
5 Make sure that you can point to maps or photographs on display boards without having to stretch or stand on tip-toe. Using a pointer, even just a ruler, is often easier.
6 Make sure that everyone can see the details of any model you refer to.
7 It may be helpful to run a video clip more than once.
8 Use large letters when writing on a flipchart or board.
9 Try to avoid turning your back on your audience for more than a few moments at a time.

> ### *Using an overhead projector (OHP)*
> - If you have never used an OHP it is worthwhile getting your tutor or a technician to show you how it works and for you to get some practice in preparing OHP acetate transparencies.
> - Make sure your writing is large enough to be seen at the back of the room and make sure you don't put too much information on to the transparency.
> - Always focus the projector before you start your talk.
> - Don't get between the screen and the projector.
> - Always point to the transparency and not to the screen.
> - Switch off the projector when you are not using it.

▶ You can produce transparencies using a photocopier by photocopying from paper originals on to special acetates.

 Planning for your audio-visuals

Go back to the plan you prepared earlier, and identify where and how you will use audio-visuals.

Being aware of non-verbal communication

Until now we have concentrated on different structures and styles of presentations, emphasizing the different ways in which you can prepare your presentation to increase your chances of communicating successfully with your audience. However, human beings don't just communicate through language; we also communicate non-verbally. Moreover, non-verbal communication is not something we can choose to do or not to do; it inevitably forms part of giving and receiving information. By non-verbal communication we mean the whole range of 'body language', such as voice intonation, gesture, posture, stance and facial expression. It can also include the attitude conveyed by clothes and general appearance.

As human beings, we are aware of all these social signs and signals and make sense of them in our everyday encounters. In fact we form very strong impressions of other people before we actually speak to them.

If, as presenters, we are aware of body language, we can try to ensure that we make an appropriate impression on our audience and reinforce what we say by what we do.

Non-verbal signals

What is being conveyed by the non-verbal communication of the following three presenters?

A shuffles papers and looks downwards.
B sits down, with hands in pockets and legs crossed.
C stands and speaks clearly while looking out of the window.

There are no right answers but you may have thought that A was unconfident, nervous and unsure of what he or she was doing; B, in ultra-relaxed mode, could convey an air of composure, but if this method was used while giving an oral presentation the audience might become rather bored. Have you met a C? This behaviour suggests that the speaker knows the subject but is not very interested in the audience!

When you are giving an oral presentation, it is important to convey an air of being prepared and confident. You will do this only if you *are* prepared, and there is no excuse for inadequate preparation. The better prepared you are, the more confident you will feel. You can also help yourself to *feel* confident by presenting yourself as being confident.

Public speakers and other performers such as actors are often nervous before an appearance, but 'playing the role' can help you to feel in charge of the situation. Dress tidily but in a way that feels comfortable for you. Make eye contact with your audience. Sweep your eyes around the room to make everyone feel that you are speaking to them. Move about a little while you are talking. Most importantly, make sure you have practised your presentation before the big event.

Practising the presentation

It is important not to read out a prepared speech word for word from a script. It is much better to talk to your audience using prompt cards. Talking to an audience is a skill and, like all skills, it requires practice. So, having identified your aims and objectives and given a structure to your talk, and bearing non-verbal communication in mind, you can start practising your delivery.

▶ Time yourself.

It is not easy to know how long it will take to deliver a talk and, when practising, you should time yourself. The optimum number of words spoken in a minute is between 120 and 150 – this speed is neither too fast nor too slow.

An ideal way to practise giving a presentation is by recording it with a video camera. This may not be possible due to lack of time or facilities, but if it is, you could team up with a colleague to film each other and offer constructive criticism of the result. Other ways of practising your talk are by using a tape recorder; by practising in pairs with a colleague whose opinion you value; by practising with your family; and by the age-old way of practising in front of a mirror. Treat these sessions as rehearsals. Even the most polished performer needs to rehearse.

▶ Look out for your strengths as well as your weaknesses.

You will be able to identify your shortcomings all too easily, but you should also identify what you do well. One way to help ensure that the feedback you get is constructive is for you to list areas for your practice audience to comment on.

A checklist for constructive feedback		
	Yes	No
In my talk did I:		
keep to my structure?	☐	☐

	Yes	No
maintain eye contact?	☐	☐
speak at a speed that was easy to follow?	☐	☐
speak clearly?	☐	☐
make it interesting?	☐	☐

In my talk did you:

understand what I was trying to achieve?	☐	☐
maintain your interest?	☐	☐
follow my argument?	☐	☐

Can you list two things that I did really well?
1
2

In what ways do you think I did them well?
1
2

Can you list two things that I should improve upon?
1
2

Can you suggest in what ways they could be improved?
1
2

For a successful talk, it is important to build up a rapport with your audience. One way to achieve this is by using humour. For example, you can play on your nervousness or inexperience by making a joke about it to your audience. Smiling also helps to build up a rapport, and so does making eye contact with members of the audience. You can vary your presentation by altering your pace or timing. For example, you can emphasize key points by speaking more slowly, by using pauses to give time for ideas to sink in, or by changing your voice intonation. All of these 'tricks of the trade' can help you to relax into the situation, feel in control and, importantly, keep your audience interested in what you have to say.

Dealing with nerves

Breathing exercises can be of enormous benefit in helping with nerves. You may have noticed that when you are anxious you tend to breathe more quickly and less deeply than you do normally, your heart begins to race and your chest muscles can tighten. All this of course makes you feel worse and thus more panicky and so the cycle keeps going.

Try some slow, deep breathing. Find somewhere quiet, close your eyes and concentrate on your breathing. Breathe in through your nose while counting to five, hold for a count of five and then breathe out through your mouth for a count of five. Repeat this several times.

Once you start speaking you will probably find that you stop feeling nervous as the adrenaline gets pumping and you become

► There are relaxation exercises that can help you to control your nervousness and that can be useful at other stressful times. Yoga can help you to become aware of your body and to 'centre' yourself and use potentially negative emotions in a positive way. The Alexander Technique is a method of improving body posture that can also have a significant effect upon well-being.

absorbed in the moment. If you do feel you are getting out of breath while talking, fit in some pauses where you can catch your breath and regain your equilibrium.

Projecting your voice

You must make sure that you can be heard by everyone. You can do this if you address your remarks to the person at the very back of the room. At the beginning of a presentation it is worth checking that everyone can hear by asking: 'Can everyone hear me?' Practise raising your voice as much as you can without actually shouting.

Planning for audience participation

What is the audience going to be doing while you are talking? You hope that it will be listening to you. But how long will you be able to hold its attention without giving it something else to do? If your presentation lasts for longer than ten minutes it is a good idea to give the audience something more to do than just listening and looking. You can ask questions, such as:

> 'Can anyone give another example of that?'

> 'Does anybody disagree with that?'

Or you can offer the audience an opportunity to ask you questions:

> 'Are there any questions at this point?'

► If you offer the audience opportunities to ask questions, remember you are in charge of the time, and you have the right to stop the question session.

Or you can take an instant 'straw poll' by inviting a show of hands by those who agree or disagree with a particular point you have made. Perhaps you could distribute a very short questionnaire for members of your audience to complete, and then discuss their answers.

It is a good idea to invite some audience participation early in your presentation. This improves rapport, and gives you a feel for the audience.

 Planning for audience participation

> Now write your ideas for audience participation into the plan you are making for your presentation.

Structuring the physical environment

Having structured your talk, chosen your visual aids and practised your presentation, you should arrive well prepared at the venue for the talk. But you're not really ready until you have checked out the room you will be using. Make sure you arrive early (or better still, check out the venue in advance) and ensure that you are at ease in the environment. If your audience is to gain the maximum interest from your talk then everyone needs to feel comfortable and not be too hot or too cold; people need to be able to see you; and they need to be able to hear you. You should therefore ensure that the chairs are arranged so that both you and the audience feel comfortable. Experiment with opening windows – is there traffic noise? If so, what can you do about it? (Move away from the windows? Change rooms?) Don't be afraid to move furniture or possible obstacles – this is *your* presentation.

Whatever you do, make sure that you and your audience feel comfortable with the environment before you start to speak. You could begin your talk by asking if the people can hear you at the back, or asking if your audience is warm enough. This is a good way to practise hearing your own voice before you give your presentation, and showing your concern for the audience sets the scene for the development of rapport.

 Checklist for equipment

Make a checklist of the equipment you will need for your presentation, such as prompt cards, transparencies, marker pens, a watch and an extension lead. Keep this checklist with your presentation plan.

Identifying strategies for evaluation

If you have identified clear aims and objectives, your evaluation will already have a good framework. You must establish how far your audience has attained the objectives. But how you find this out is more difficult. You could design an evaluation questionnaire that you place on each chair before your audience comes in and that you mention during your talk. This will provide you with some quantifiable data about the success or otherwise of your talk. If you choose this method, try to ensure that the questions you use are easy to understand and address your objectives. It would be a good idea to discuss this questionnaire with your tutor before using it. You could use a modified version of the checklist on pages 180–1.

Another way to gauge audience reaction is to include some questions in your talk so that you can give your audience a chance to engage in debate. Another method is to leave some time at the end of your talk for a short question-and-answer session.

One of the most useful ways of evaluating an oral presentation is for you to write a one-page critical evaluation of your own performance, perhaps based on the responses to the audience questionnaire. To make this self-evaluation exercise valuable, you should use this opportunity to develop your critical skills. Don't just ask: 'How did it go' or 'How did I feel about it', but ask questions that require careful answers, such as: 'Why did that work?', 'Why did I feel nervous?', 'How could I have used the visual aids in a better way?', 'What was unclear about my structure?' 'When did I begin to feel in command of the situation and why?'

Such critical self-reflection could be included in the final report of your research as evidence of your developing skills of evaluation and self-awareness.

▶ Further detail about managing question-and-answer sessions is included under the seminar section on pp. 184–7.

Presenting as a group

Giving a presentation as a group requires considerable planning and rehearsal in advance. Everyone must know what he or she is going to do, and know what everyone else is going to do. Preparing and giving a group presentation is an excellent way of practising teamwork, and is often used to assess this valuable skill.

Guidelines for presenting as a group
- Hold regular planning meetings throughout the research period.
- Leave enough time for the final planning meeting and rehearsal.
- Work out the timescale of the presentation with accurate deadlines.
- Be clear about who is going to present each part and what each person is going to say.
- Be clear about who is responsible for different aspects of the presentation (introducing, summarizing, managing the visual aids).
- Agree in advance how you will evaluate the presentation.

GIVING A SEMINAR

A seminar is a specialized kind of oral presentation. If you are asked to participate in or lead a seminar, make sure that you understand what the term 'seminar' means, since it is used in a number of different ways. Within an educational setting a seminar usually means a semi-formal paper on an academic subject that an individual or a small group delivers to the remainder of a small group of fellow students. The paper to be presented is usually handed out at least a week before the seminar to give the whole group a chance to read it and to do any other prior reading. After the paper has been presented at the seminar, the seminar presenter or presenters lead a discussion during which the group discusses the content of the paper.

Seminar groups vary in size but a typical group would comprise around a dozen students and a tutor. An important difference between giving an oral presentation and delivering a seminar paper is that with a seminar paper you will be expected not simply to answer questions but also to lead a discussion and defend the arguments put forward in your paper.

Typical length

The length of a seminar varies, but it is unlikely that you would be asked to present for longer than twenty minutes. However you should discuss this with your tutor. The length of discussion could be between thirty minutes and an hour and a half. Again, discuss this with your tutor.

Writing the seminar paper

The main points referred to in the previous section, on identifying aims and objectives and developing a structure for a talk, apply equally to the development of a seminar paper. You should identify the aims and objectives for the paper, and then write the paper in a similar way to an essay, i.e. with an introduction, a main body of argument and a conclusion. A seminar paper should come with a list of questions to be considered and possibly one or two references, or key readings, that the seminar participants can read before the meeting.

Having written your seminar paper and distributed it to your peers, the typical way to 'give' a seminar paper is to 'talk to it'. This means that you will not merely read it out (after all, the participants will have had it for at least a week and should have read it through carefully). Talking to a seminar paper means that you will identify the main points that you have put forward and discuss them, perhaps using visual aids, and develop them for the group. You may want to relate your argument to the general work that the group has been doing so that it is put into context. You could be challenging or controversial (a good way to get discussion going!) or pose problems and potential solutions as a way of generating discussion.

Leading a discussion

Your job as leader of the seminar is to promote discussion of the contents of the seminar paper. You are not there to dominate the discussion but to 'manage' it. Equally, you do not have to defend your paper in every detail. The purpose of the discussion is for everyone to learn from it, and this includes you. Don't be afraid to say 'I am having problems with this part of the work. Can anyone help?'. If someone points out that you have made a mistake, look on this as a help to you rather than a negative criticism, even if it sounds like one.

For the purposes of leading the discussion, you are effectively in the role of tutor. This may be very exciting or very scary, but if the tutor is still in the room you can expect it to be potentially problematic. You should establish from the outset what role your tutor expects you to play. If you're leading the group, will you have to deal with any unruly behaviour or will your tutor deal with this? Who is responsible for closing the whole session?

Members of the group

Though the leader is responsible for the seminar paper and for managing the discussion, the members of the group have responsibilities as well. They should have paid the presenter the courtesy of reading the paper in advance and carrying out any identified reading. They should be willing to participate in discussion. This is easier if some work has been carried out on developing a good atmosphere in the group so that members know each other and feel comfortable about speaking in that forum. If the group members do not already know each other, you could suggest that members of the group in turn give their name and area of interest. There is a wide range of 'ice breaker' activities that could be used to help a new group to relax – in Further Reading we suggest some books that would be valuable for this. However, your tutor may well have already done some work in this area.

Handling tricky situations

Be reassured: you can learn to lead a discussion and to deal with tricky situations.

Don't be afraid of silences. Silences are often very creative and, although it can be difficult not to jump in to fill the gap, if you hold on and maintain the silence, the group will have a better chance of taking full ownership of the discussion.

What if you are asked a question you can't answer? This happens to all of us – the trick here is to recognize these moments as opportunities for group learning. You could respond by saying 'That's an interesting question, but I'm not sure of the answer. Does anyone have any ideas?'. In this way you are giving the opportunity for solution to the group.

The same is true if someone is trying to put you in a difficult position by being provocative or rude. You could again use the group, perhaps by asking for other comments: 'That's one view, what do the rest of you think?'

Evaluating a seminar

There are two main parts to a seminar: the paper and the discussion. They should be evaluated both separately and together. As always, evaluation should be done with reference to the aims and objectives you set yourself at the start.

The evaluation of the paper can be carried out using a modified version of the checklist on page 168. The evaluation of the discussion and of your leadership of it overlaps with this as far as other students' learning is concerned, but you should also prepare a list of objectives for the discussion. You could then evaluate your leadership with a modified version of the audience questionnaire on pages 180–1.

Taking part in a discussion

▶ The specifications for Communication Core Skills in GNVQ contain detailed criteria about taking part in discussions. If you are taking a GNVQ course, make sure that you are familiar with these criteria.

The particular combinations of personalities in a group play a large part in shaping the discussions of that group. There may be people who dominate the group discussion and others who say very little. There may be those who are more concerned with the image they are presenting than with the subject matter in hand. When people take part in a group discussion they may be trying not to appear naïve, over-confident, over-clever or aggressive, while at the same time trying to be witty, intelligent and attractive. It is important to remember that each member of a group influences how that group operates, even if he or she does so by remaining silent. The success or failure of a discussion group largely depends on whether everyone takes responsibility for how the group operates and whether people feel free to contribute. This group dynamic will develop as individuals get to know each other and feel less embarrassed about speaking out, but it can take some time and the group leader must encourage it.

Talking and listening skills

As a group member it is important to listen carefully to the contributions of others as well as contributing yourself. Achieving this balance requires practice.

To be an effective group participant you should consider the following possibilities:

- Listen closely for most of the time, occasionally contributing a carefully thought-out remark or question to clarify what is being said.
- Attempt to paraphrase, or sum up, what someone else has said to ensure that you have understood the point that person was making.
- Ask questions that begin with phrases such as: 'Do you mean that . . . ?', 'What do you think about . . . ?' or 'How do you think that will develop . . . ?'
- Comment in response to someone who has just spoken.
- Express support for an idea that someone else has put forward.

By contributing in these ways you are helping the group to clarify ideas, and you are learning for yourself as well as helping to shape the group dynamic in a challenging and supportive way. If you have prepared for the discussion you will already have your own ideas and questions to contribute. If you are leading the discussion, the group is there to help sort out your ideas. Either way, groups can offer positive learning opportunities for all members.

Further reading

Sandra Ashman and Alan George (1982) *Study and Learn*, Oxford: Heinemann.

Bill Jones and Roy Johnson (1990) *Making the Grade*, Vols I and II, Manchester: Manchester University Press.

CHAPTER SUMMARY

This chapter has explored strategies for planning and delivering oral presentations. It has considered ways in which presenters might:

- develop a structure and aims and objectives for their talk;
- identify and use appropriate visual aids;
- organize the physical environment;
- select appropriate styles of presentation;
- be aware of non-verbal communication;
- evaluate their performance.

The chapter also explored ways in which seminars can be presented, including identifying strategies for leading a discussion, and emphasized the importance of contributing to discussions.

What to do when things go wrong

SOMETHING ALWAYS GOES WRONG

There are two main reasons why students are required to do research as part of their course. The first is that it is easier to understand and remember things that you find out for yourself than things that you are told about. The second is that it provides an opportunity to develop and to demonstrate the skills of research and enquiry that are needed in almost every occupation that you are likely to follow. In many cases, the second of these reasons is the more important, and it is the one that this book is concerned with.

▶ For student projects, the process of doing research is at least as important as the outcome.

Remember, however, that one of the rules of all research is that:

Something will always go wrong.

This is as true for the experienced and distinguished researcher, in any field, as it is for the student. Research projects have many pitfalls and unforeseen problems will always arise. However, there is an old saying that there are no problems, only opportunities. Difficulties that occur during your project create an opportunity for you to learn from the challenges you face, to find solutions and to evaluate those solutions. In all courses, but particularly in GNVQ courses, the skills you show in handling information and in responding to problems are assessed and will contribute to your final grade.

If you have followed the advice given in this book then you should have avoided most of the problems that regularly confront student researchers in their projects. This chapter gives further suggestions about things to avoid and solutions to problems. When problems arise, face them calmly and remember that you can usually rely on support from your tutor or your fellow students – but you will have to ask for it; don't expect your tutor to guess that you have a problem.

▶ There is often more than one solution to a problem. The key is to select the solution that is most feasible.

UNEXPECTED RESULTS

Unexpected results are more likely to occur in explanatory research than in descriptive research. If you have an unexpected result, or you find that something unexpected is happening in a situation, make sure that you have the evidence to support any claim you make in your final report. Check your calculations. Look out for pieces of data that are particularly surprising, and then, if you can confirm them from your records, offer an explanation. Never change your evidence to suit your conclusions. Don't be frightened to come up with something new or different, but do be very sure of your evidence and your calculations.

NO RESULTS

You may find that all your hard work on data collection and analysis produces no results that you can report. What are the possible explanations? It may be that you have left out some important questions, or asked questions that did not prompt interesting or relevant answers. If this happens, make the best of the situation by doing an evaluation and critique of your methods and making recommendations for better ways of designing the research in the future. You will get credit for this since you are showing that you understand the *processes* of research and that you can stand back and evaluate your own work.

If your problem is that you couldn't gain access to the people or the places you needed to study, you could write a report about the difficulties of gaining access for research, using your experiences as evidence.

If your problem is that your research participants now won't allow you to use the data they have given you, you could change your project into a case study of the ethics and problems of confidentiality in research.

Generally, if you have 'no result', explain and evaluate the situation and make some recommendations for a different strategy for the same research. In some cases, you might argue that 'no result' is a valid result, and that the subject matter of your enquiry is unresearchable.

▶ Negotiate a code of conduct with research participants early in your project.

NEEDING SUPPORT

The amount and type of support you will need depends both on the kind of project you are doing and on your own strengths and weaknesses. Unfortunately, the tutor–student relationship can sometimes be a troubled one. The most common reason for this is that the roles and expectations of each person are not made clear.

At an early stage of the research, ask for clear guidance about what support you can expect from your tutor and what your tutor expects from you. A constructive and thorough way to do this is to develop a 'Student's Charter'. This should specify exactly what sort of help you are entitled to and how often, and should set out what obligations you have to your tutor. It is best to develop this jointly with your tutor.

Student's Charter (sample extract)
- The tutor and the student will meet every two weeks for a half-hour tutorial at a prearranged time.
- The student will submit sections of work at least three days before each tutorial.
- The student will receive written feedback on all written work that has been submitted within two weeks of its being submitted.
- If either student or tutor is unable to meet a deadline, fair warning of this will be given.

A Student's Charter can be developed at any time during your project, though it is best to agree one from the start. A group of students with the same tutor could develop a Charter that is common to them all.

Valuable support can also be gained from friends and fellow researchers. Students doing similar projects will experience similar concerns and encounter similar problems. Informal meetings with fellow students can provide interesting and appropriate support. This kind of mutual support may be essential and is often the most easily available, but it requires everybody to contribute. No one should be allowed to ask for help but never have to give it.

► Make use of peer group support.

Don't wait until the last minute to hand in what you have written. You will usually find that tutors are willing to read draft sections of your report early on and to give you some feedback. It may be part of your Charter that this will be done. Pay careful attention to the feedback and act on it. If there are a lot of comments written on the draft, or if you take a lot of notes from spoken feedback, it can be a bit daunting. It is often helpful to analyse the points that your tutor has made, to number them, and then to deal with them one by one.

► On the whole, the students who need most support are the ones least likely to seek it. Is this you?

PROBLEMS WITH INFORMATION

Information and resource materials are not always readily available and are sometimes difficult to locate, especially at short notice. If vital information is unobtainable at the time it is needed, don't be afraid to change your plans and, if necessary, to change your topic. This is not unusual, even among very senior researchers.

If you have taken the advice in Chapter 8, you will have completed a search for relevant sources as early as you can. In a small project you cannot possibly read everything so you will have to be very selective – you may need advice on this. Some publications may not be available in your usual library. You could try another one or you might use the interlibrary loan facility. Remember that interlibrary loans are expensive, so choose your requirements very carefully and order things in good time. When you read an interlibrary loan book that you have to return, take careful notes of what you need from it. Also note the complete reference (author, title, publisher, etc., see pp. 164–5), because once it is returned it has in effect gone for ever from your project. You are allowed to take one photocopy of each of a limited number of pages of a book, provided that you use them only for personal study.

If you have lost a reference or the source of a quotation, there is not much you can do about it and, if it is not vital, it is best not to use the quotation. Under no circumstances should you quote from someone else's work without giving that person recognition. If you did this you would, in effect, be passing it off as your own work. This is plagiarism, and it can get you into serious trouble (see Chapter 11, p. 166).

▶ Don't throw anything away unless you have kept at least one copy of it.

▶ Never tamper with your original tapes or notes. If you do need to do anything with them, then make a copy and use that.

Just remember, never throw anything away until well after the project has been completed. Keep all tapes and field notes. Keep copies of all results from experiments, all diagrams and all documents. You never know whether you are going to want to refer to them again. You may find that something you don't need in an early chapter becomes unexpectedly useful in a later chapter. You may wish to get your tutor or a colleague to listen to your tapes for confirmation. You may need to find a piece of evidence or a reference at the last minute.

Your tutor will advise you how long to keep your raw data. This may be only until you are sure the project has been assessed. It may be longer, especially where you are going to do follow-up research. Occasionally you can take old data and look at it in a new way, so it is worth keeping it.

PROBLEMS WITH COMPUTER TECHNOLOGY

It is very likely that you will use a computer in your project, for example using a word-processor to write your report. Whether you are using a computer to store information, to make calculations, or to write up your project,

Save! Save! and Save!

Always keep a second copy of your disk.
Always keep an up-to-date hard copy (print-out of your text).
If you have problems with computer software, seek advice from staff who are knowledgeable about computers and with that particular software package. If your disk becomes damaged or 'corrupted', seek assistance from an expert. Computer personnel, such as technicians, may be able to recover your information. If the computer 'hangs up' in the middle of your work, get expert help. Unless you are really certain that you can solve the problem, get help rather than trying to retrieve the situation yourself.

Check that you are using the most appropriate computer statistics, graphics or word-processing package, or whatever. If in doubt, check with your tutor.

Always leave time to learn a new package. At least in the early stages, it is usually better to attend a short course than to try to teach yourself from the manual.

LOW RESPONSE RATES

► For help with computer hardware and with printers, you should seek advice from a computer technician.

You may find that you are not getting enough replies to your questionnaires or to your letters asking for information. In the case of letters to organizations, try telephoning to check that your letter was addressed to the right person, then send one polite reminder and, if it is really important, follow this up with a phone call to the person concerned. If none of this works, forget it and try another source. Don't wait indefinitely. The information may never come.

In the case of postal questionnaires, there is generally a good response at first and then returns slow down. Inevitably, not all questionnaires will be returned by the specified date. There are various possible responses to this problem.

You can, if you have the time and the money, send a second letter and questionnaire. This is possible if you had devised a system of numbering that allows you to identify respondents. However, if you had promised anonymity, there would be no way of linking responses or non-responses with individuals, so it would not be possible to send reminders and second questionnaires.

You could try replacing the 'lost' data by sending out questionnaires to new people, but this may threaten the representativeness of your sample (see Chapter 6, pp. 80–1), since the replacements may not match the originals.

You could collect additional data through personal interviews, which are designed to collect the same data as would have come from your postal questionnaire. These semi-structured interviews, using a small sample of your original target group, could also provide further and more in-depth data for your project, and could add greater validity to your original data.

Remember, however, that many large-scale postal questionnaires sent out to strangers often achieve a response rate of less than 20 per cent. Though you are likely to send questionnaires to a closer and smaller group, don't expect very high rates of response.

PROBLEMS OF RESEARCHER BIAS

As you interact with the participants in your study, a number of biases can creep in. Sometimes your expectations and desire for particular results can distort your perception of the situation, your judgement and therefore your results. You may treat ambiguous situations as unambiguous and assume that they are the way you

► If you influence your participants so that they behave in the way you predicted they would behave, this is referred to as the **Pygmalion Effect**. When your personal bias leads you to see only the evidence that you want and expect to see, this is called the **Procrustean Effect** (see p. 150).

► **Bias**: an error that is always in the same direction; a systematic error. For example, a bathroom scale that always registers five pounds too light is biased because it systematically distorts all weighings the same way.

want them to be. You may simply not see or hear things that don't match your expectations. Obviously this will lead to results that are biased in the direction of your expectations.

Knowing that you should be on the look-out for biases is of little help if you don't know exactly what to look for. The problem is that any research variable can become a bias. Which ones are and which ones are not depends upon what is being studied and how the study is being conducted. For example, the gender of the interviewer can be a source of bias in a study about equal opportunities for men and women. However it would not necessarily influence answers to questions about teachers' salaries. Similarly, failing to promise anonymity would surely bias an enquiry into criminal activity but is unlikely to affect people's willingness to tell you where they went to school.

Bias exists to some degree in every study, but the presence of bias does not imply that the study should be totally discredited. Some biases can safely be ignored because they are either irrelevant or too small. The ethnic origins of the drivers are irrelevant, for example, to a study of the most cost-efficient long-distance routes for heavy lorries.

While it is not possible to eliminate all potential sources of bias, careful research design will eliminate the major ones. Bias only becomes a major problem when it affects the results of your study.

You may need to discuss the issue of potential bias with your tutor. It should always be taken into account in your research design.

> ### Bias from unrepresentative samples
> One of the commonest ways in which bias enters a research study is through an unrepresentative sample. In Chapter 6 we gave you advice about how to deal with representativeness in retrospect (see p. 95).

If you are concerned about bias in your study you will need to assess the effect that this bias is likely to have on your project. You will need to ask: 'How will this bias affect the observations made or the results of the study?' If bias becomes apparent later in the research process or during the writing up of the report, refer to it and evaluate its importance when you draw your conclusions.

It is usually helpful to ask other students or your tutors to give their views, especially on how far they think the bias you have identified will affect your results.

► Remember that potential sources of bias might not have an effect, either because they are too small to matter or because your research design has eliminated them.

PROBLEMS OF PARTICIPANT BIAS

How certain can you be, when you are doing projects that involve people, that you are getting a true picture from them? It is important to be aware of situations where things may not be quite as they seem.

Never underestimate people's desire to give the answer that they think you want to hear or that they think will be the most helpful to you or flattering to themselves or their organization. Never underestimate the effect that an 'authority' figure can have. You may not feel very authoritative, but in an interview you are in charge and this can bias people's answers. Even if you are not authoritative, most people will still tend to give you answers that will conceal their faults or weaknesses.

Leading questions

Consider this question about honesty:

> Please choose option A, B, or C:
>
> If I found a purse containing a large amount of money in the street I would:
>
> A   leave it where it was
>
> B   hand it in to the police
>
> C   consider it a lucky find

Which one of these answers is the most socially desirable response? Can you think of any way to encourage people to be really truthful in their answer?

Surveys on smoking among the young can run into this problem. Since some young smokers may do so partly as a way of raising their self-esteem, they might overstate the amount that they smoke. On the other hand, quite the opposite can happen. One researcher did a project on television watching and asked young people to estimate the number of hours a week they spend watching television. Can you think of reasons why they might wish to state fewer hours than they do actually watch? Can you think of any way of finding out the 'true' figure?

Reactivity

Participants in a research project may behave differently because they know they are being researched. This is known as **reactivity**, and it can arise in any experiment or observation that involves people, whether this is conducted in a laboratory or in a more natural setting. The key question is whether the people in the experiment are behaving as they would normally or whether their behaviour is at least partly influenced by the knowledge that they are part of an experiment and are being observed.

As a researcher, you must continually ask yourself: 'Are these people behaving differently from usual just because I am giving them attention?' This question has recently been asked in a case where researchers claimed that children with reading difficulties have become better readers after sessions where they sit for twenty minutes at a time staring at flashing coloured lights. Others have

▶ The **Hawthorne Effect** was first identified and studied in the 1920s at the Hawthorne Works of the Bell Telephone Company. It was found that the behaviour of participants in the study was being influenced by their knowledge that they were being observed.

questioned this finding as a possible example of the Hawthorne Effect. Do children become better readers because of all the attention they are getting?

You may be aware of the use of 'placebos' in tests for new drugs (see Chapter 4, pp. 47–8). One group of people is given the real drug and another group is given the placebo – a pill or capsule that looks like the real drug but is a harmless substitute – both groups are told that they are getting the same drug. If the two groups have different responses, then it is likely that the drug is the cause. If such an experiment were carried out by giving the drug to one group and nothing to the other, any benefit experienced by people in the first group might be because they *believed* the drug was beneficial.

There is also the possibility of a reaction that is the opposite of the Hawthorne Effect. Suppose an experiment takes place in which the people in one group have nothing done to them (the control group) while those in another group have something done (the experimental group), and then both groups have to perform a task. People in the control group may feel: 'This is not fair, I'll show them!', and may end up performing better than the experimental group.

It is important to remember that when you are observing people your presence can affect their behaviour. You cannot do very much about this except try to be as unobtrusive as possible, by adopting the following tactics:

- Say as little as you can.
- Don't say things that you think may influence them – such as giving *your* opinions.
- Be careful who you are seen with. If people see you talking frequently with their superior, for example, they may think you are talking about them and they may be less willing to give you the data you want.
- Don't talk about people to others in the group – everything you hear from one person must be confidential. If you are discovered to have revealed something said to you in confidence, you may find that people (and not only the person whose confidence you betrayed) are unwilling to be open with you.

▶ The kind of person you are will have an effect on the people you study. People's answers to your questions may vary according to your age, your clothing, your hairstyle, your ethnic group, your accent and so on, and according to how much they share the same characteristics.

So what can you do if, halfway through your research, you realize that your presence has had an effect on a situation? The only solution is to acknowledge this in your report, and try to make a judgement of how much this may have affected your findings.

TOO MANY WORDS

You have been shown in Chapter 10 how to plan to stay within a word limit. The example given there was for a project of 2,000 words. Whatever your word limit, you can work out a similar plan.

If you plan carefully, and stick to the plan, you can keep within your limit. But what can you do if you find that you are going way beyond it? Here are some suggestions:

- First, identify how many words you have to cut. If it is only a handful, you can find these a few at a time. If major cuts are needed, deleting a few words or even sentences will not be enough. You will have to cut paragraphs, pages, and whole sections. Once you know your target for cuts, keep a tally of your progress towards that target.
- Go back to your original statement of the purpose of your research and read it again.
- Then read your report section by section. Identify the key points in each section that relate to the original purpose and the paragraphs and sentences that make those points. How much of what is left can you cut? Remember, you have to cut something, so the less important material must be the first target. Are there parts you could leave out altogether without changing the quality or the meaning of what you have written? How much of what you have written is not central to the main purpose of your research?
- Have you described something in words that you could have represented in a diagram or a flow chart? Look again at Chapter 10 for examples.
- Have you included in the main text material that could be taken out and placed in an appendix to your report?

▶ Condensing your writing into a much shorter version is called writing a **précis**. You may be able to get further advice on this from a Communications textbook or a Communications tutor.

RUNNING OUT OF TIME

The final problem, and one that affects everyone, is time. The important point is that there is no cure for running out of time. Finishing a report by writing through the night before the deadline day will not produce successful results. The only real solution is to avoid the problem in the first place. Prevention is better than cure.

▶ Do it now. There won't be time tomorrow.

Try very hard to resist the tendency, which everybody has, to put things off to another day. Get going with the organization of that data as soon as you can. Don't put it off. Plan (as in Chapter 7, p. 100) to have a series of target dates within your overall schedule.

For some people, the hardest thing to get down to is the writing of the report. There is only one answer to that – start writing. Don't wait for the perfect conditions or the right mood. You can always go over it again. Nearly everybody writes more than one draft.

> ### *If you really have run out of time*
> If, despite all this, you really do run out of time, there are two things to do, and in this order.
>
> 1 Reduce the scale of your research project.

Focus your questions more tightly. Concentrate on only part

► In putting together a rescue package like this, pay close attention to the assessment specifications so that you can salvage whatever will score most marks.

of what you intended to do. Analyse only some of the questions on the questionnaire. In short, try to make a viable project out of less. You will get a lower grade, but that is better than the nothing you will get if you miss the final deadline altogether.

2 Investigate whether you can negotiate an extension to your deadline.

You should know about this from your Student's Charter. However, if the deadlines are clearly stated in the course regulations, don't expect much sympathy unless your problem arises from illness or some domestic problem.

LEARNING FROM DISASTERS

If you are feeling gloomy about the results of your research, remember that you are doing this work mainly to learn about doing research. Your assessment will be loaded more towards rewarding you for what you have learned about doing research than towards the importance of your results. This means that while your project may turn out to be a disaster as research, you may still be able to pass the assessment by evaluating your work and showing what you have learned from the disaster.

CHAPTER SUMMARY

In this chapter we have looked at some of the pitfalls to avoid and how to retrieve situations when you fall into them. We have emphasized throughout that, in the last resort, student research is set and assessed mainly for what the student has learned from doing it. That means that it is possible to foul up the research and still pass the assessment.

Index